# UNDERSTANDING

# CORBA

## (Common Object Request Broker Architecture)

**Randy Otte, Paul Patrick and Mark Roy**

For book and bookstore information

http://www.prenhall.com

**Prentice Hall PTR**
**Upper Saddle River, New Jersey 07458**

Library of Congress Cataloging-in-Publication Data
Otte, Randy,
   Understanding CORBA : the common object request broker architecture /
Randy Otte, Paul Patrick and Mark Roy
      p. cm.
   Includes index.
   ISBN 0-13-459884-9
      1. Object-oriented programming (Computer science) 2. Application software.
   3. Electronic data processing--Distributed processing. I. Patrick, Paul. II. Roy, Mark.   III. Title.
QA76.64.088   1996
005.7--dc20                                             95-37455
                                                        CIP

Editorial/production supervision: *Joanne Anzalone*
Manufacturing manager: *Alexis R. Heydt*
Acquisitions editor: *Mark Taub*
Editorial assistant: *Dori Steinhauff*
Cover design: *Scott Weiss*
Cover design director: *Jerry Votta*

© 1996 by Prentice Hall PTR
Prentice-Hall, Inc.
A Simon & Schuster Company
Upper Saddle River, New Jersey 07458

The publisher offers discounts on this book when ordered in bulk quantities.
For more information, contact: Corporate Sales Department; Prentice Hall PTR; 1 Lake Street, Upper Saddle River, NJ 07458
Phone: 800-382-3419, Fax: 201-236-7141
E-mail: corpsales@prenhall.com

Printed in the United States of America
10 9 8 7 6 5 4 3 2

# ISBN 0-13-459884-9

Prentice-Hall International (UK) Limited, *London*
Prentice-Hall of Australia Pty. Limited, *Sydney*
Prentice-Hall Canada Inc., *Toronto*
Prentice-Hall Hispanoamericana, S.A., *Mexico*
Prentice-Hall of India Private Limited, *New Delhi*
Prentice-Hall of Japan, Inc., *Tokyo*
Simon & Schuster Asia Pte. Ltd., *Singapore*
Editora Prentice-Hall do Brasil, Ltda., *Rio de Janeiro*

## In Memoriam

To Mike Renzullo, a valued friend, colleague, and one of the original architects of Digital's CORBA implementation, who passed away during the writing of this book.

# Contents

## 2 A Conceptual Overview of CORBA

## 3 An Architectural Overview of CORBA

## Part II  For the Application Designer: Designing a CORBA Application Framework

# 4 Designing a CORBA Application

# 5 Refining Your Object Model

# 6 Considerations in Distributing Your Design

# 7  Coding with OMG IDL

# Part III  For the Application Developer: Developing a CORBA Application Framework

# 8  Developing the Client Side of the Application

# 9 Developing the Server Side of the Application

**B  Names of CORBA Operations and Objects for Versions 1.1 and 1.2**

**C  CORBA Standard Exceptions**

**D  Summary of Operations for Dynamic Invocation**

**Glossary**

**Index**

**Examples**

# Figures

## Tables

# Preface

## Audience

If you are reading this book, you are likely to be either a person interested in what exactly CORBA is all about in general terms or a person interested in the details of designing, developing and deploying a distributed application using CORBA.

If you are interested in general knowledge about CORBA, such as its relationships to other standards, how it came about, and what its components are, then Part I is for you.

If you are an application designer or developer interested in the details of how to create a distributed application with CORBA, then the entire book is of interest to you. Parts II, III, and IV, respectively, discuss how to design, build, and deploy a distributed CORBA application.

In writing this book, we did not assume that you as a reader are experienced with using object-oriented programming, are familiar with CORBA or the work of the OMG, or are familiar with any particular software vendor's CORBA system.

## Typographic Conventions

This book uses the following conventions:

| Symbol | Meaning |
|---|---|
| **bold text** | indicates the introduction of a new term that is defined in the glossary. |
| `monospaced text` | indicates code fragments, routines, operations, constructs, or attributes. |

| Symbol | Meaning |
|---|---|
| . . . | indicates one of the following conditions: |
| | • Optional arguments omitted. |
| | • The preceding item or items can be repeated one or more times. |
| | • Additional parameters, values, or other information can be entered. |
| .<br>.<br>. | indicates the omission of items from a code example or command format that are not relevant to the topic being discussed. |
| [ ] | in examples, indicates that whatever is enclosed in the brackets is optional; you can select none, one, or all of the choices. |

# Source Code Conventions in the Examples

The OMG IDL and C source code examples in this book use the following conventions:

| Coding Convention | Description |
|---|---|
| /* OMG IDL */ or<br>/* C */ comment | Comments at the beginning of substantial code fragments indicate the programming language (OMG IDL and C code are very similar in appearance). |
| {<br>} | Braces delineate the beginning and end of a piece of code and have the same left-side indentation as the code the braces delineate. |
| MODULENAMES | Module names are in uppercase text and do not contain underscores. By not allowing underscores in the module name, we can distinguish the names of nested modules from the names of non-nested modules. For example, the Module B contained within Module A would be named A_B. If underscores were allowed in module names, nested module and non-nested module names could conflict. CORP is a valid module name. |
| operation_names | Operation names in the OMG IDL language are in lowercase text and contain underscores between words in the operation name. For example, promote is a valid single-word operation name. |
| argument_names | Argument names are in lowercase and can contain underscores to separate words in the name. For example, new_job_class is a valid argument name. |

| Coding Convention | Description |
| --- | --- |
| CONSTANTS and ENUMERATED_TYPE_ MEMBER_NAMES | Constants and enumerated type member names are in uppercase letters and words in the names are separated by underscores. For example, HIRED_HOURLY is a valid enumerated type member name. |
| UserDefinedTypeNames | User-defined type names are in mixed case and do not contain underscores. Each word in the variable name has an initial uppercase letter; other letters in the word are lowercase letters. User-defined types are created using structures, typedefs, interfaces, attributes, and so on. For example, DeptInfo is a valid user-defined type name. |
| non user defined data type names | Non-user-defined data type names are in lowercase and cannot contain underscores to separate words in the name, but can use spaces. For example, unsigned long is a valid data type name. |
| CORBA_C_bindings | CORBA C bindings of non-user-defined OMG IDL data type names are prefixed with CORBA_. Although this is not a convention used in Version 1.1 of the CORBA specification, it is part of the Version 1.2 specification and so we adopted it in this book. For example, the CORBA data type that corresponds to the C long data type is CORBA_long. |

# Diagram Conventions

The following conventions are used in the diagrams in the book:

Indicates a computer system or group of computer systems.

Indicates a CORBA component. The use of multiple boxes offset from each other indicates that there may be more than one copy of that component, such as multiple client applications.

Indicates components and interfaces that are conceptual and in some cases end user-supplied, such as the OMG IDL code.

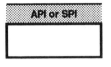 Indicates an application programming interface (API) or system programming interface (SPI) that CORBA defines. These interfaces conceptually sit on the physical components that implement or contain them (for example, the object adapters implement the BOA API).

 Indicates components and interfaces defined by the CORBA architecture.

Indicates components and interfaces that are not defined by the CORBA architecture, but that are related to it.

## Related Documentation

The following is a list of related books that you might find useful, grouped by the topics they cover:

- Distributed computing

  - *Distributed Computing Implementation and Management Strategies* edited by Raman Khanna, published by Prentice-Hall (ISBN: 0–13–220138–0)

- CORBA and the Object Management Group (OMG)

  - *Object Management Architecture Guide* by the OMG

  - *The Common Object Request Broker: Architecture and Specification* by the OMG

  - *Common Object Services Specification, Volume I* by the OMG (ISBN 0–471–07684–8)

  You can obtain copies of specifications from OMG over the Internet through the File Transfer Protocol (FTP) with the following address: ftp.omg.org.

- Distributed Computing Environment (DCE)

  - *Understanding DCE* by Ward Rosenberry, David Kenney and Gerry Fisher, published by O'Reilly & Associates, Inc. (ISBN: 1–56592–005–8)

  - *Guide to Writing DCE Applications* by John Shirley, published by O'Reilly & Associates, Inc. (ISBN: 1–56592–004–X)

- Object-oriented analysis and design

  - *Object-Oriented Analysis and Design with Applications* by Grady Booch, published by Benjamin/Cummings Publishing Co (ISBN: 0805353402)

- *Object-Oriented Analysis and Design* by James Martin and James J. Odell, published by Prentice-Hall (ISBN: 0–13–630245–9)

- *Object-Oriented Software Construction* by Bertrand Meyer, published by Prentice-Hall (ISBN: 0–13–629049–3)

- *Designing Object-Oriented Software* by Rebecca Wirfs-Brock, Brian Wilkerson, and Lauren Weiner, published by Prentice-Hall (ISBN: 0–13–629825–7)

- Digital's ObjectBroker product, which implements CORBA

  - *ObjectBroker Overview and Glossary*

  - *ObjectBroker Installation and Configuration Guide*

  - *ObjectBroker System Integrator's Guide*

  - *ObjectBroker Reference Manual*

These documents are available through Digital Equipment Corporation (telephone number: 1–800–DIGITAL).

# Acknowledgments

This book would not have been possible without the work and support of many people, not the least of whom are our families, who wondered if our work on this book would ever be finished.

First and foremost, we need to thank Steve Baron and Pat Carney from Digital Equipment Corporation who gave us the time to do the work on this project, and the folks at Prentice Hall who liked what we produced well enough to publish it.

A special thanks goes to Pat Srite who took the book in its final stages and distilled it into what we are publishing today with Prentice Hall.

In addition, we are thankful for the following folks who either took the time to review portions of the book, or helped in other ways: Neal Jacobson, Dr. Daniel Frantz, Paul Reilly, Mary Jane Grinham, Gary Schmitt, Evelyn McKay, Susan Hunziker, and Michelle Chambers.

# Part I

## An Introduction to CORBA

Part I introduces CORBA, where it came from, and what its benefits are to you as a software designer or software developer. Part I includes the following chapters:

- Chapter 1 introduces CORBA, describing what problems it solves and how CORBA is a marriage of distributed computing and an object model.

- Chapter 2 provides an overview of key CORBA concepts, including definitions of terms and related object-oriented concepts.

- Chapter 3 provides an architectural overview of a CORBA system, which includes an architectural diagram and an explanation of the CORBA components and interfaces.

# 1

# Why Use CORBA?

In the business world today, users need to share information across enterprises as never before. The reasons for this are as varied as the businesses that use computers. Information to be shared comes from many sources. Today, there are thousands of standalone applications on dozens of hardware and software configurations—few of which are designed to share information or communicate with any other applications on their own platforms, let alone with applications on differing platforms. If an application does share information with other applications, it can typically talk to only a few select applications.

Integrating these applications and systems is not easy. Computers from different manufacturers often use different data formats (16-bit, 32-bit, or 64-bit). In addition, byte ordering often differs between systems, requiring special converters to enable data sharing between differing systems.

Tying together this jumble of applications running on a variety of hardware and software configurations often requires a custom solution. This solution can be time-consuming and expensive because of the number of different applications that need to be connected. And if six months later another application or platform needs to be tied into the custom environment, even more time and money will need to be spent in integrating that application or platform.

Users of these systems must cope daily with the limitations of their computing environments. The following scenarios show several typical problems resulting from a lack of application and systems integration:

• **An engineering firm has information from a variety of sources.** The engineering firm needs to share information from sources as diverse as the advertising department's graphics applications, the finance department's PC spreadsheets, and the engineering department's workstation-based CAD/CAM applications. Managers want to work in their favorite PC spreadsheets and simply pull in the data they need from these sources over the network, including both current and historical data.

## Why Use CORBA?

- **A large manufacturing company has systems that have been evolving over decades.** The company has mainframes, minicomputers, and personal computers with local area networks (LANs), wide area networks (WANs), and multiple database management systems. They also have a diverse set of applications on a variety of platforms, such as CAD/CAM applications on UNIX systems, a workflow control application on an OpenVMS system, and production information applications running on Microsoft Windows systems. The company wants to integrate these different work elements so they can leverage existing hardware and software as part of the solution to their next business problem. There are frequent changes in the software environment, due to new business needs, introduction of new technologies, and organizational changes.

- **A small city bank has merged its systems with a larger banking institution.** The merger of the two banks has left the larger bank with a multitude of information access problems. For example, bank tellers are dealing with multiple applications and databases to do simple tasks, such as getting a customer balance on several accounts, and customers are waiting far too long to get information. The bank wants to integrate the existing applications and systems so employees can quickly and efficiently access information from multiple sources. The bank also wants to build new applications to be as simple as possible and to be extensible so there is no need to rewrite them later.

- **An investment company must work with changing information from many sources.** The investment company deals daily with real-time information about prices of securities, world changes, historical pricing information, market and industry trends, and information on existing portfolios that the company handles. All this information is stored in relational databases on mainframes. The company is using software from a dozen different vendors and that software is running on several different hardware platforms. Financial planners are spending far too much time accessing and merging data for all their reports and customer contacts.

**CORBA**, the Common Object Request Broker Architecture, can help to address these problems. CORBA lends itself well to solving the problems encountered in integrating legacy applications and systems as well as providing the flexibility for dynamically changing business environments.

## 1.1 What Is CORBA?

CORBA is a specification for a standard object-oriented architecture for applications. CORBA was first defined by the Object Management Group (OMG) in the *Object Management Architecture Guide*, a document published by the OMG in November 1990. The OMG is a nonprofit organization founded in 1989 and currently has over 500 members. The OMG is dedicated to popularizing object-oriented standards for integrating applications based on existing technology.

The published definition of CORBA is contained in *The Common Object Request Broker: Architecture and Specification*. Version 1.1 of this specification, published in December 1991, describes how to develop a CORBA implementation. Version 1.1 was jointly developed by Digital Equipment Corporation, Hewlett-Packard Company, HyperDesk Corporation, NCR Corporation, Object Design, Inc., and SunSoft, Inc. and reviewed and accepted by all of the OMG.

There are two updates to the CORBA specification in process: Version 1.2 and Version 2.0. Both updates are in draft stage and were not formally published at the time of this writing. The OMG expects to publish the Version 2.0 specification in June 1995. Version 2.0 will incorporate the changes made in both Versions 1.2 and 2.0. This book is based on the Version 1.2 specification.

You can obtain a copy of the draft specifications using ftp (see the Preface for ordering information).

## 1.2 What Problems Does CORBA Solve?

The major problem enterprises face today is the need to integrate a multitude of different work elements, so the enterprise can use existing hardware and software to solve current and future business problems. A significant part of this problem is integrating existing applications on mainframes with newer desktop environments. Creating solutions from scratch is too costly and time consuming.

You can use CORBA to address these problems. With CORBA, you can connect personal computers and their applications with the rest of the enterprise without interfering with the existing hardware, network, and software infrastructure. CORBA provides the ability to:

- Access distributed information and resources from within popular desktop applications.

- Make existing business data and systems available as network resources.

- Augment popular desktop tools and applications with custom functions and capabilities for a particular business.

- Change and evolve network-based systems to reflect new topologies or new resources.

## 1.3 CORBA Is Based on Distributed Object Computing

The integration of applications in a CORBA environment is based on an object-oriented model. This model provides anaylsis, design, and implementation techniques for building software that is extensible, reusable, and less costly to produce and maintain than function-oriented software.

An implementation of CORBA provides the basis for developing the next generation of software, which is the development of reusable software. Just as we now plug and unplug disk drives and memory boards, we are near to the point where we can plug and unplug networks, class libraries, and applications. The ability to reuse software is now commercially available through distributed object-oriented systems like those that implement CORBA and through other new object-oriented technologies, such as C++ class libraries.

CORBA makes the reuse of software possible through **distributed object computing**, which combines the concepts of distributed computing with object-oriented computing. There are two essential ingredients of distributed object computing:

- The marriage of distributed computing with an object model

  CORBA is an excellent marriage of distributed computing with an object model. Each partner not only brings to the match its own fine qualities but also complements the qualities of the other. CORBA enables applications to access and share each other's objects, in effect making these objects common to all applications that implement CORBA.

- The use of a broker

  CORBA uses a **broker**, or intermediary, to handle messages (called **requests**) between clients and servers in the system. The broker provides the ability to choose servers to best fill the client's request and separates the **interface** that the client sees from the implementation of the server. (An **implementation** is the software that actually accomplishes a client's request for an operation on an object.) This separation lends itself well to producing a flexible, building-block approach where you can hide changes to the server from the client. Given that you do not modify the interface and its behaviors, you can create a new server or modify an existing server without changing the clients.

The following sections provide more detail on the concepts of distributed computing, object models, and brokers and their application in CORBA.

# 1.4 What Is Distributed Computing?

Simply put, distributed computing is two or more pieces of software sharing information with each other. These two pieces of software could be running on the same computer or on different computers connected to the same network. Most distributed computing is based on a **client/server** model. With the client/server model, there are two major types of software: **client** software, which requests the information or service, and **server** software, which provides the information or service.

## 1.4.1 Benefits of Distributed Computing

The primary benefit of distributed computing is the ability to use computing resources more efficiently through the use of techniques, such as:

* Sharing of scarce resources. For example, if you have only one high-quality printer or only one plotter of a certain type, distributed computing lets you make that printer or plotter available to everyone on your network and not just to those with accounts on the machine connected to the printer or plotter.

* Parceling out computing workload among many different machines.

* Putting applications on the machines most appropriate to their needs.

Sharing scarce resources and parceling out workloads are some of the core ideas behind computer upsizing and computer downsizing, which are techniques for moving from nondistributed computing to distributed computing. **Computer upsizing** is the process of moving your business from nondistributed computing on individual personal computers to networked distributed computing that includes individual personal computers, high-performance servers, and workstations. **Computer downsizing** is the process of moving your business from nondistributed computing on mainframe computers in computer labs to distributed computing among workstations and personal computers in your offices.

## 1.4.2 Existing Mechanisms for Distributed Computing

In addition to CORBA, there are two other common ways to build distributed solutions:

* Using remote procedure call (**RPC**) mechanisms

* Coding to a network application programming interface (**API**)

The use of these methods, however, detracts from the primary task of developing a solution to a business problem; that is, when using RPC or a network API you must deal with infrastructure issues in addition to solving the business problem.

Distributed computing tends to focus on RPC mechanisms to distribute applications across the network. As its name implies, RPC deals with procedure calls. Procedures are typically **synchronous** in nature, which means the requesting application must wait while the server performs the procedure. Applications using RPC must often be aware of some aspects of network transports and are responsible for locating servers that can satisfy requests. In addition, RPC often requires servers to be active when the request is initiated, which limits where a request can be serviced. DCE RPC allows the specification of multiple servers, but the application programmer must discover those multiple servers and choose one. DCE RPC does not have a broker to handle automatic discovery and routing to servers.

Although network APIs can support both synchronous and **asynchronous communication**, they provide no services to encode data so that applications on platforms with different representations of data can understand the data.

Using network APIs frequently requires you to create and work with additional software, which is often very low-level software that you should not have to bother with, such as software dealing with the data representation differences on different platforms. To create this software, you might have to answer such questions as how to convert a floating point on a personal computer to a floating point on a VAX system. You also have to write code to package and deliver requests, as well as to unpack and deliver them to the routines. You are likely to do a lot of manipulation of buffers and be concerned with subtleties between different platforms.

## 1.4.3 How CORBA Enhances Distributed Computing

CORBA enhances the use of distributed (client/server) computing by:

- Allowing a flexible, changing relationship between clients and servers
- Adding an intermediary, called a broker
- Allowing servers to be more than single processes
- Supporting both synchronous and asynchronous communication styles

The following sections provide more information on these enhancements.

### 1.4.3.1 CORBA Allows a Flexible Client/Server Relationship

In traditional client/server terminology, a client and a server have a fixed relationship. That is, the client always makes the request for a task to be performed and the server always performs the requested task.

CORBA allows this same relationship between the client and server as well as other more flexible relationships. In fact, with CORBA, a piece of software that acts as a client for one request might act as a server for the next request. This flexibility is a by-product of CORBA's object-oriented approach.

For example, suppose there are two pieces of software in a CORBA system: a viewer that allows you to display graphics or documents of various types and a print manager that allows you to select and print files. The end user starts the viewer and tells it to display a document and then to print the file it is displaying. The viewer sends a request to the print manager to print the file. In this case, the viewer is requesting a service and so is acting as a client, and the print manager is providing a service and so is acting as a server. This is illustrated in Figure 1–1.

**Figure 1–1  Viewer Software Acting As a Client**

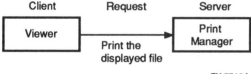

ZK-7718A

Now let's add an electronic mail system to our example so we can see how the viewer can act as both a client and a server. The electronic mail system delivers a mail message that contains an embedded graphic to an end user. When the end user attempts to read the message, the mail system examines the message, finds that the message is in a format that it cannot display, and sends a request to the viewer to display the message for it. For this request, the mail system is a client requesting a service and the viewer is a server providing a service.

The viewer displays the embedded graphic and the end user requests a printout of the graphic, so the viewer calls the print manager as before. For this request, the viewer is a client requesting a service and the print manager is a server providing a service. Figure 1–2 illustrates this example.

**Figure 1–2  Viewer Software Acting As Both a Client and a Server**

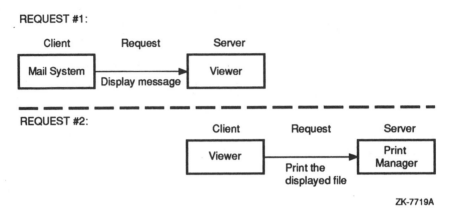

ZK-7719A

### 1.4.3.2  CORBA Adds a Broker

In a traditional client/server environment, there is a one-to-one relationship between the clients and servers. CORBA adds a new layer between the client and server: a broker. The broker provides the intelligence necessary to map abstract service requests from the client to particular server implementations. Recall that, while DCE RPC allows the specification of multiple servers, DCE RPC does not have a broker to handle automatic discovery and routing to servers.

Figure 1–3 shows the insertion of the broker into a traditional client/server environment.

**Figure 1–3  Insertion of a Broker In a Client/Server Environment**

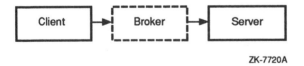

ZK-7720A

The addition of the broker results in several enhancements:

- CORBA clients and servers do not need direct knowledge of each other.
  CORBA clients and servers find each other through the broker, rather than knowing directly about each other. This way, only the broker needs to know the locations and capabilities of the CORBA clients and servers on the network, and so the clients or the servers, themselves, do not need to contain this information.

- CORBA does not require a one-to-one relationship between clients and servers.

  A traditional client/server environment has a one-to-one relationship between clients and servers. With the insertion of the broker in CORBA, multiple servers can work with a single client or a single server can work with multiple clients as shown in Figure 1–4.

**Figure 1–4  Multiple Clients and Servers with a Broker**

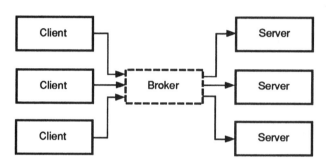

ZK-7721A

- CORBA client applications can locate and interact with new objects and servers at run time.

  In a traditional client/server environment, invocation of requests is predefined. That is, there is a set procedure for clients to make requests of servers. With CORBA, client applications can also invoke requests on objects dynamically at run time.

### 1.4.3.3  CORBA Servers Can Be More Than Single Processes

In a traditional client/server environment, developers think of the client and the server as single processes. With CORBA, this is not necessarily true. Although CORBA clients are typically single processes, servers might or might not be single processes. A CORBA server can be any of the following:

- A single process

- An intermediary server that requests other servers to perform the tasks the client requests

- A shareable piece of code, such as a library that is dynamically loaded at run time, which the application process calls, rather than the server being a process itself

### 1.4.3.4 CORBA Supports Both Synchronous and Asynchronous Communication Styles

Synchronous communication is when one piece of software sends a message to another piece of software and then waits for a reply. Asynchronous communication is when one piece of software sends a message to another piece of software and then continues working, expecting the reply to come at some later time. CORBA calls its asynchronous communication style **deferred synchronous**. CORBA's definition of asynchronous communication is actually a polling model where the client inquires whether an operation has completed. CORBA also defines **one-way** requests, in which the application does not need to wait for completion of the request, but there are no return arguments.

There are advantages and disadvantages to both synchronous and asynchronous communications styles. Most client/server environments support only synchronous communication. Rather than supporting one style or the other, CORBA provides both communication styles to the CORBA software developer.

## 1.5 What Is an Object Model?

An object model is a concept of object-oriented computing. In a broad sense, an object model is a conceptual framework for thinking about a problem and its possible solutions. The basis for the object model is the fundamental concept of **objects**, which are entities that exhibit specific behavior and have attributes. Objects are entities of the real world; for example, a car is an object, as is a hammer, a process, or an employee. Objects provide the means for combining behavior and attributes into a single entity. Attributes enable you to get or set data for an object. Objects can have operations performed on them. An **operation** identifies an action that can be performed on an object, given a specified set of arguments. Each object can only be manipulated through the operations defined for that object.

An object model builds on the following object-oriented concepts:

- Abstraction

  **Abstraction** is the ability to group objects and focus on the common characteristics of the group. For example, a city map abstracts details of a city and shows only those details, such as streets and major buildings like schools, churches, and fire stations. If a city map included all buildings, the map would lose its usefulness. Different types of maps, such as road maps or topological maps, abstract different details. In object-oriented design, developers use abstraction to decompose a system into groups of objects, which can be further abstracted. This enables developers to focus on what can be done with the objects, rather than on the implementation details. Each object has a specific role in the system and connects to other objects.

- Encapsulation

  **Encapsulation** hides the implementation details of an object from the services it can provide. When you use encapsulation in the context of an entire application, you hide how an object works from the rest of the system. Other objects can request services by sending messages to the object that provides the service. Encapsulation enables you to modify an object's implementation without affecting its clients and to write client applications more easily.

- Inheritance

  **Inheritance** allows you to pass along the capabilities and behaviors of one object to another object. When an object inherits behaviors from a single interface, it is called single inheritance. When an object inherits behaviors from more than one interface, it is called multiple inheritance. Not all object-oriented systems support multiple inheritance.

- Polymorphism

  **Polymorphism** is the ability to substitute objects with matching interfaces for one another at run time. That is, you can give a common description to objects that share the same behavior and properties. CORBA calls this description an interface. With polymorphism, instances of objects that have a common description can respond to the same request using different actions. Polymorphism makes it possible to design applications that are easily extensible. Not all object systems use or require polymorphism; CORBA requires it.

## 1.5.1 Advantages of Using an Object Model

The use of an object model allows developers and designers to:

- Define a system model based on the real world.

  Using an object model, you can build your software based on the real world once you make decisions on such things as the problem domain you are working in, the objects you want to define and the attributes and behaviors they have, and what relationships the objects have with each other.

- Logically separate a system into objects that can perform certain tasks called operations.

  Because each object can perform only certain operations, it is very clear both to the designer and to the developer what each object can be used for. For example, a bank teller object might be able to perform only deposit and withdrawal operations. Defining the parts of your system into objects and operations results in fewer errors in your software because you must clearly define the operations that each object supports. This makes the interactions between the objects much smoother and better understood. In addition, the software is more modular, so you can work on software components independently because there are fewer dependencies among objects in the system.

- Extend the model as requirements change.

    As requirements change, it is not difficult to change well-designed software in an object-oriented system. If you already have all of the objects that are necessary in your domain, new requirements probably mean only adding new behavior on a particular object and putting existing objects together in new and useful ways. Adding new requirements is not likely to result in new relationships; it often requires only extensions to the objects you already have in place. In contrast, with a function-oriented model, adding new requirements could cause a redesign of major portions of the system.

## 1.5.2 Advantages of CORBA's Incorporation of an Object Model

Because CORBA uses an object model, CORBA views all the applications in the CORBA system as nothing more than a collection of objects and associated operations. The location of the underlying application on the network and the operating system on which the underlying application runs is transparent to the client.

For example, a system built using CORBA might connect an advertising department's graphics applications, a finance department's PC spreadsheets, and an engineering department's CAD/CAM packages. These applications are all represented as objects in CORBA. In reality, developers usually define objects so that each application is represented as several different operations on several different objects. Because all CORBA objects have an agreed-upon method of communication (sending requests through the broker), any object can potentially provide and receive information from any other object. For example, the engineering department might share a CAD/CAM drawing with the advertising department.

CORBA's object-oriented model provides several benefits that make it easier to integrate applications into a distributed system. Some of the advantages of using CORBA's object-oriented architecture and approach include the ability to do the following:

- Use object-oriented design techniques in creating your system.

    Object-oriented design concentrates on how to abstract the parts of a system into objects that interact with each other. Object-oriented design techniques encourage the designer to define each object in the system as a component that is capable of performing certain tasks without the system requiring knowledge about how that component accomplishes those tasks.

A good example of such a component approach to design is a component stereo system. Each component has jacks for input, for output, or for both. You can use these jacks to connect all the components together to play music without any of the components requiring knowledge about the internal circuitry of the others. In a similar way, you can connect a set of software objects by operations to perform some action.

- Reuse more software.

  CORBA's object-oriented system promotes the reuse of objects and the object-oriented concept of inheritance. Objects are self-contained, which makes them easy to reuse—you just connect their interfaces into your new application and use them. For example, if you have a set of objects written to handle tax computations for one application, you can easily reuse them for another application.

  Inheritance promotes software reuse by allowing one object to subsume the capabilities and behaviors of another object. For example, suppose your software must handle two categories of employees: bank tellers and loan officers. Your software handles these two categories of employees the same way, except that the software includes added capabilities for the loan officers to approve and disapprove loans.

  In CORBA, you could have the loan officer object inherit the capabilities and behaviors of the bank teller object. If the operations on the bank teller object change, the system automatically makes the same changes for the loan officer object because it inherits from the bank teller object.

- Use familiar programming languages.

  CORBA is not an object-based system that requires its own language, such as Smalltalk, Trellis, or Eiffel. Instead CORBA allows you to create an object-oriented system using more familiar programming languages, such as C, C++, and even COBOL.

# 1.6 How Distributed Computing and an Object Model Complement Each Other

The combination of distributed computing and an object model in CORBA enhances both distributed computing and object-oriented computing.

CORBA adds the following to these environments:

- Distributed computing enhancements

  To a distributed computing environment, CORBA adds references to particular objects in the environment. To perform operations in CORBA, all you need to do is ask an object to perform the operations it can perform. For example, if you have a reference to an account object, you can request deposit and withdraw operations. A client developer does not need to know any more information.

- Object model enhancements

  To an object model, CORBA adds the concept of a broker. The broker allows applications to interact without the applications knowing where other applications are on the network or how they accomplish their tasks. A client sends a request to the broker asking that a certain operation be performed on an object. Only the broker needs to know the locations of CORBA clients and servers on the network.

  CORBA's incorporation of an object model provides an excellent way to abstract some of the inherent complexities of the client/server environment. Object-oriented computing complements the benefits of distributed computing because it hides object brokering functions, such as finding out if there is a server, locating the server, and determining how to get to the server. The CORBA object request broker also solves some of the problems of calling from one application language to another language (for example, C++, Smalltalk), from one object model to another object model, and even from object-oriented systems to non-object-oriented legacy systems.

## 1.7 CORBA Is Communications Middleware

**Middleware** is software that resides between an application and the inner workings of the system hosting the application. Middleware insulates applications from the lower-level details and complexities of the software on which the system depends so the application developer has only to deal with a single API of some sort—the middleware handles the other details. Instead of coding to operating system or low-level interfaces, the application developer can use the middleware to work on a higher level in the application, while the middleware provides the lower-level details.

For example, with database middleware, the developer can code to one interface, such as the structured query language (SQL) or the open database connectivity (ODBC) interface, and thereby access dozens of different vendors' databases on dozens of different platforms. There are other middleware services that handle the complexities of user interfaces, such as Motif,

X Window System, or Presentation Manager, which free developers from dealing directly with user interfaces.

CORBA has been called communications middleware because you can view CORBA as software that insulates an application from the details of the communications kernel. However, software developed according to the CORBA specification does not necessarily need to communicate over a network. It could result in a method that is contained in the client's own address space.

# 1.8 CORBA and the Distributed Computing Environment

CORBA is a specification for one kind of distributed computing; it is often compared to another popular system for distributed computing developed by the Open Software Foundation (OSF) called the Distributed Computing Environment (DCE). At first glance, both CORBA and DCE seem very similar because both are specifications for middleware. Because both CORBA and DCE are designed to provide a middleware solution, vendor implementations of each have tended to provide similar functions, such as a client/server communication mechanism, a way to handle security and authentication, a way for clients to find servers, and so on.

As both CORBA and DCE change over time, they will probably become even more similar in function as each incorporates new technologies that improve its own distributed computing system. Because the features of both systems are so similar, the real difference between CORBA and DCE is not in the features that each provides, but in the underlying distribution model that each uses and the communication styles those distribution models support.

## 1.8.1 Comparing the CORBA and DCE Distribution Models

The DCE distribution model is based on its RPC software and uses a procedure-oriented distribution model. The CORBA distribution model is based on the use of objects and uses an object-oriented distribution model.

RPC has no inherent object model in it. If you want the benefits of an object-oriented technology, you must add constructs and mechanisms to the base RPC technology. With CORBA, instead of adding your own object-oriented technology on top of RPC, you get a mechanism that has an object model built in and that enables distributed computing.

In DCE, application clients invoke procedures that the RPC maps to a corresponding function in a server. DCE clients need a fairly low-level knowledge of how to use RPC to connect to application servers. For example, each client needs to know what servers are available to it and the exact RPC call needed to access that server.

In CORBA, application clients do not connect directly to servers as they do with an RPC. Instead, CORBA clients send requests to the object request broker, which then directs those requests to a server that can perform the requested task.

By using an object request broker to separate the client and server, CORBA lets developers operate at a higher, more abstract level of programming than the more traditional model that DCE uses. In addition, because clients and servers are not hard-wired into each other in a CORBA system, the system is more flexible. With CORBA, it is possible to add servers that client applications can use without changing any code in the client applications themselves, or to add new clients that use existing servers. By contrast, in a DCE system, developers must change the client code whenever the client wants to take advantage of any new server functions.

### 1.8.2 Comparing Communication Style Support

Both CORBA and DCE support synchronous communication between clients and servers. However, only CORBA allows the additional use of asynchronous communication in a nonthreaded application. DCE provides asynchronous communications through the use of multiple synchronous threads in an application, which execute concurrently.

Because CORBA supports synchronous and asynchronous communication styles without requiring you to program in threads, CORBA is better suited to the encapsulation of non-threaded legacy applications that need the flexibility of asynchronous communication. For example, if you have an asynchronous C program running on a mainframe system and you want to add it to your DCE system, you need to rewrite that program to either be synchronous or to use threads. Either approach could be a time-consuming task.

If, on the other hand, you want to take this same program and add it to your CORBA system, you need only to wrap this application so that it appears to the object request broker as a CORBA implementation on a server. Any CORBA client can then make requests of this implementation. This is much easier to do than rewriting the legacy application, and you can do it without modifying a line of code from the legacy application.

### 1.8.3 Summarizing the Differences

CORBA is likely to be a better choice for you than DCE if:

- Your distributed computing system will need to be extended or modified.

- You need asynchronous communication without using threads.

- You want the benefits of object-oriented analysis and design.

However, DCE is likely a better choice for you than CORBA if:

- You want the integrated suite of services that DCE provides.

- You do not need the capabilities of an object-oriented system.

Either DCE or CORBA would be a good choice if your system is very stable and unlikely to change or if you do not need asynchronous communication.

For more information on DCE and other topics related to CORBA, see the Preface in the book for a list of related documentation.

# 1.9 What is the OMG Object Management Architecture?

The OMG *Object Management Architecture Guide,* published in November 1990, defined an object-oriented architecture for applications called the Object Management Architecture (OMA), which is the basis for CORBA.

The OMG OMA consists of four components shown in Figure 1–5 and defined as follows:

**Figure 1–5   The Four Parts of the Object Management Architecture**

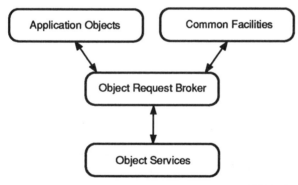

ZK-7722A

- Object Request Broker

  The Object Request Broker (ORB) is the component from which CORBA derives its name. The ORB provides the communication hub for all objects in the system. The ORB's function is analogous to that of a hardware bus, in that it provides the path taken by all information that flows between objects.

Because the ORB is central to the other OMA components, the ORB was the first component that the OMG specified and that software vendors have implemented. The OMG first publicly described the ORB component in *The Common Object Request Broker: Architecture and Specification* Version 1.1 in December 1991.

• Object services

The object services provide a set of standard functions to create objects, control access to objects, track objects and object references, and so on. The object services are essentially a set of system services for objects developed to benefit the application developer. The object services allow application developers to call object service functions instead of writing and calling their own private object service functions.

The member companies of the OMG are currently working on specifying the object services and have published a specification for the first of these services in the *Common Object Services Specification, Volume I* (COSS 1). COSS 1 is the first in a series of specifications designed to complement and extend CORBA and aid in standardizing distributed systems. COSS 1 includes specifications for the following object services: object naming (for locating objects), object events (for conveying events between objects), object life cycle (for control of object creation), and the persistent object service (for storing objects).

• Common facilities

The OMG is currently developing specifications for common facilities. Common facilities provide a set of general-purpose application capabilities for use by many different applications, such as facilities for compound document management, accessing databases, printing files, or synchronizing time in a distributed environment.

The member companies of the OMG are currently working on specifying the common facilities needed.

• Application objects

Application objects provide a set of objects that perform specific tasks for end users. These are essentially object-oriented applications. You can build application objects using other more basic objects, some of them specific to a particular application object and some taken from the common facilities. For example, you could build a word processing application object using application-specific objects to handle the creation and manipulation of a document, and common facility objects to handle the printing and storage of a document.

Software vendors might provide application objects. The OMG has not standardized these objects.

# 1.10 What is the Current Status of CORBA?

The OMG is building the CORBA standard from the inside out, standardizing first the basic support, then the interface, and so on. Because CORBA gives vendors considerable leeway in system-dependent aspects, this book describes how vendors might have interpreted the specification.

Both Versions 1.2 and 2.0 of the CORBA specification have been written, but they are currently in draft stage and not formally published. The OMG expects to publish the Version 2.0 specification in June 1995 at which time this specification will override both the Version 1.1 and Version 1.2 specifications.

The Version 1.2 specification clarifies a few minor points in the Version 1.1 specification and also specifies that all CORBA-defined names be scoped as if they occurred in the module CORBA. For example, the Version 1.1 BOA_create operation becomes the CORBA_BOA_create operation in Version 1.2. See Appendix B for a list of the differences in the names between versions.

The Version 2.0 specification addresses several issues not covered in the Version 1.2 specification, most notably how to handle communication and interoperability between different vendors' ORBs. CORBA currently specifies a definition language and language bindings for client applications. The Version 2.0 specification will have a small amount of change in the C bindings for memory management purposes.

The following companies were involved in the initial specification of CORBA and are now developing, or have delivered, full or partial implementations of CORBA: Digital Equipment Corporation, Hewlett-Packard Company, International Business Machines Corporation, IONA Technologies, and SunSoft. There are a few other companies also developing CORBA implementations.

# 1.11 Where Is CORBA Headed?

Given the large membership of the OMG and its drive toward the development of CORBA, the CORBA specification is approaching the status of a standard.

Future CORBA specifications will define standards for server development. Several standards currently under development, such as the Fresco X Toolkit, are declaring themselves to be CORBA compliant, as are various applications being built on top of various CORBA systems.

The ORB was the first component of the OMA model that the OMG specified. The OMG has now also specified various object services and common facilities components for the OMA model as well as language bindings for C++ and Smalltalk. The OMG is working on additional programming language bindings for LISP and COBOL, and others to supplement the language bindings (C, C++, and Smalltalk) described in the current specification. Both the C++ and Smalltalk bindings are not yet published.

In addition to the work being done to extend CORBA, the OMG published the first listing of object service specifications in COSS 1 in March 1994. This document includes specifications for an object service naming service, event service, life cycle services, and object persistence services. In the near future, it is expected that various vendors will provide these services, just as various vendors have provided implementations of CORBA. Volume II of COSS has been approved and will be published shortly. Volume II includes concurrency control, externalization, relationship, and transaction servers.

The member companies of the OMG will continue to develop specifications for new object services as they are needed. Some of the object services being worked on now that might appear in a future volume of the object services specification are licensing, query, change management (versioning), and security (access control).

# 2

## A Conceptual Overview of CORBA

This chapter explains some of the concepts and terms associated with CORBA.

## 2.1 CORBA Formally Separates the Client and Server

A distributed computing system has client processes and server processes running on computers and communicating using some network protocol. In most distributed systems, the clients request servers to perform some functions and the servers perform those functions. In these systems, it is often the case that the clients and the servers are closely linked so that each knows a great deal about how the other does its job. Initially, this might make it is easier to build this type of system, but it means that you cannot subsequently change the client or server without changing the other.

With CORBA, the client and the server are formally separated so that you can change one without changing the other. A CORBA client knows only how to ask for something to be done and a CORBA server knows only how to accomplish a task that a client has requested it to do. This means that you can change the way a server accomplishes a task without affecting how the client asks for the server to accomplish that task. For example, you can can evolve and create brand-new implementations of a CORBA server and never change the client or you can create new clients that make use of interfaces from existing CORBA servers without changing the servers.

CORBA's formal separation of clients from servers is very similar to the separation of a procedure from a calling program in structured programming. Think of the client as the main part of a program and a server as the procedure that it calls. The program (client) calls the procedure (server) to write some information, and the procedure then writes the information. Information on how the procedure actually accomplishes the writing of the information to the device is kept internal to the procedure. The calling program does not need to know how the job is done; it only needs to know how to call the procedure that does the work. Similarly, a client using a CORBA object-oriented interface does not need to know how the server accomplishes its task; it only needs to know how to request that an operation be performed on an object.

## 2.2 Requests

CORBA separates the client and server by restricting communication between the client and the server to a type of message called a request. Every interaction in a CORBA system is based on a client sending a request or a server responding to a request. The process of sending a request is called **invocation**.

All requests have the same basic form and consist of the following parts:

- An indication of the operation for the server to perform at the request of the client.

- A reference to a specific object on which to perform the operation.

- A mechanism to return exception information about the success or failure of a request.

- An optional reference to a **context object**, which might contain additional information to be propagated from the client to the server as part of the request.

- Zero or more arguments specific to the operation being requested.

For example, an object might be an employee and promoting an employee might be an operation on that object. In this example, the request is the message sent from a client to the server to perform the promote operation on a specific instance of an employee object.

## 2.3 OMG Interface Definition Language

With any distributed application, the client and server need basic information to be able to communicate, such as information about the available operations the client can request and the arguments to the operations. CORBA includes this information in an interface. In CORBA, an interface defines the characteristics and behavior of a kind of object, including the operations that the server can perform on those objects. If you are familiar with object-oriented terminology, an interface is similar to a class.

To define interfaces in CORBA, you use the Object Management Group (OMG) Interface Definition Language **IDL** to code the information into a set of **interface definitions**. Developers capture these interface definitions in OMG **IDL files**. Before you can write a CORBA client or server application, you must first create or access an OMG IDL file or interface repository that contains the definitions of interfaces the client or server implementation will support.

## 2.4 OMG IDL File

An OMG IDL file describes the data types, operations, and objects that the client can use to make a request and that a server must provide for an implementation of a given object. For example, an OMG IDL file could describe an employee interface that defines the promote and dismiss operations and a user-defined data type and a constant. A client application that made use of this OMG IDL file would be able to make requests for the promote and dismiss operations and use the specified data types and constants. A server that could satisfy requests from this client must be able to do the work associated with performing the promote and dismiss operations and handle the specified data types and constants.

OMG IDL is a definition language and not a programming language. You use OMG IDL to define interfaces and data structures, but not to write algorithms. You can use the OMG IDL file to generate source code for the desired programming languages.

The use of a definition language such as OMG IDL frees CORBA from being restricted to any particular programming language. This is an important benefit of CORBA because being tied to a particular programming language has been a common problem for object-oriented systems in the past. Currently, the OMG has defined language bindings for C, C++, and Smalltalk. OMG member companies are developing proposals for other language bindings, such as LISP and COBOL. As the OMG approves these language bindings and various CORBA vendors include them into their systems, you will be able to develop CORBA clients or servers independent of one another in the language that best fits your needs. That is, you could write the client in LISP and the server in C.

Example 2–1 shows a portion of an interface definition in OMG IDL. This interface is part of a sample distributed personnel application that maintains employee data for a corporation. In Example 2–1, the OMG IDL code defines two operations for the employee interface: promote and dismiss. This means that if a client uses the employee interface, the client can request that a server promote or dismiss a specific instance of an employee object.

For more information on coding with OMG IDL, see Chapter 7.

Example 2–1  A Sample OMG IDL Interface Definition

```
interface Employee
    {
    void promote  (in char          new_job_class);
    void dismiss  (in DismissalCode  reason,
                   in string         description);
    };
```

## 2.5 Object Instances and References

An **instance** is a specific occurrence of an object and a term used in object-oriented systems to indicate that something is a specific case of a more general category. For example, the employee, Dave Smith, is a specific instance of the employee object, and the chair Dave sits in is a specific instance of the general concept of a chair object. Dave cannot sit in the concept of a chair, but needs a real, physical instance of a chair. When we talk about objects, we are usually talking about instances of objects that are actually used in the system.

To identify specific instances of objects to the CORBA system, you use an **object reference** to that instance. For example, a client requesting the promote operation on a specific employee object would identify that object by specifying its object reference as part of the request. The internal representation of an object reference might differ, depending on the CORBA vendor's implementation of the system. Regardless, all object references have the same external representation for a given language. This makes an application portable across different vendor systems.

Because CORBA systems pass object references instead of specific objects, application developers can use programming languages that are not object-oriented and also use a different programming language for the client application and server application.

## 2.6 Implementation of an Object

An implementation of an object is the part of a server application that satisfies a client's request for operations on a specific object. An **object's implementation** (referred to as an implementation in the remainder of this book) exists in a server application and contains one or more **methods**, which are the pieces of code that do the work requested of the implementation. For example, if a client requests a promote operation on a specific employee, the implementation uses its method to do the job of promoting that particular employee.

Figure 2–1 illustrates a client application and a server application, which is capable of performing operations on employee objects. The client application has acquired an object reference to a specific employee object, Dave Smith. Because this object is an instance of an employee object, it supports the promote and dismiss operations. The server application contains an implementation of the employee object. This implementation contains the methods that will satisfy client requests for the promote and dismiss operations on an instance of an employee object, in this case, the Dave Smith object.

**Figure 2–1  A Client and an Associated Implementation on the Server**

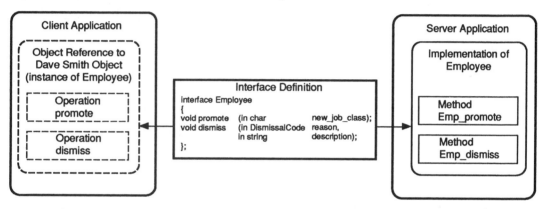

ZK-7733A

Figure 2–1 shows two operations on the client side and their related methods on the server side as follows:

- Promote operation and its related method, Emp_promote, which performs the tasks associated with promoting an employee.

- Dismiss operation and its related method, Emp_dismiss, which performs the tasks associated with dismissing an employee from the corporation.

## 2.7 Exceptions

CORBA communicates information about the success or failure of a request. CORBA refers to this information as an **exception**. All requests contain a mechanism for an implementation to return exception information as part of a request. The syntax used varies depending on the programming language being used. An implementation might provide exception information if there is an error of some kind, such as insufficient funds. The ORB itself can also raise an exception, for example if the ORB does not have the privileges to access a particular server.

The client application can read, but not enter, exception information. If there is no exception information, the request was successful. If there is exception information, the client application uses that information to determine whether to retry the request.

## 2.8 CORBA Example

Let's now go through an example using some of the CORBA terms and components introduced in this chapter.

Let's assume we have a distributed application to do administrative tasks associated with employee data in a personnel database, such as updating an employee's status (hired, promoted, dismissed, active, and so on). An end user of the client of this distributed application performs the procedure to promote an employee, D. Smith.

The steps for promoting D. Smith are as follows:

1. The end user enters D. Smith's name and department into the client application to identify D. Smith, an instance of the employee object, to the application.

2. The client application takes this information and uses it to get the object reference for the D. Smith object.

3. The client application then invokes a request with the D. Smith object to perform the `promote` operation on the D. Smith object.

   The client application's request for the `promote` operation contains certain required arguments, such as the object reference for D. Smith and the new job class. The client application can request this operation on an employee object because it knows about the employee interface, which defines how all employee objects function and what operations are valid on them (in this case, the `promote` and `dismiss` operations). This is the same employee interface shown in Example 2–1.

The ORB then locates a server that contains an implementation for employee objects. The server is started and the implementation activated if one is not available. Once the server is located, the ORB delivers the request to the implementation for processing.

4. The employee implementation executes the Emp_promote method and marks the instance of the employee object, D. Smith, as promoted in the corporate personnel database.

5. Because the operation was successful, the Emp_promote method does not raise an exception.

6. The client application displays a message to the end user that indicates the promote operation successfully completed.

# 2.9 Summary of CORBA System Concepts

Table 2–1 summarizes key CORBA concepts.

**Table 2–1  Key Concepts in a Distributed CORBA System**

| CORBA Concept | Definition |
| --- | --- |
| Client application | Invokes requests for a server to perform certain operations on certain objects. A client application uses one or more interface definitions that describe the objects and operations the client can request. A client application uses object references, not objects, to make requests. |
| Exception | Contains information that indicates whether a request was successfully performed. |
| Implementation | Defines and contains one or more methods that actually do the work associated with an object operation. A server can have one or more implementations. |
| Interface | Describes how instances of an object will behave, such as what operations are valid on those objects, and so on. You use an interface definition to describe interfaces typically using OMG IDL to code them. |
| Interface definition | Describes the operations that are available on a certain type of object. |
| Invocation | Is the process of sending a request. |

(continued on next page)

Table 2–1 (Cont.)  Key Concepts in a Distributed CORBA System

| CORBA Concept | Definition |
| --- | --- |
| Method | Is the server code that does the work associated with an operation. Methods are contained within implementations. |
| Object | Is a person, place, thing, or piece of software. An object can have operations performed on it, such as the promote operation on an employee object. |
| Object instance | Is an occurrence of one particular kind of object. For example, if an employee is an object, then D. Smith could be a particular instance of that object. Specific instances of objects are often referred to in a CORBA system using object references. |
| Object reference | Is a reference to a specific instance of an object. An object-oriented system such as CORBA usually passes around references to an object rather than passing the objects themselves. Object references are compact and the actual instances of objects can be quite large. |
| OMG Interface Definition Language (IDL) | Is a definition language for defining interfaces in CORBA. |
| Operation | Is the action that a client can request a server to perform on an instance of an object. |
| Request | Is a message sent between client and server applications. |
| Server application | Contains one or more implementations of objects and their operations. |

## 2.10 What's Next

Throughout the rest of the book, we will be using the example personnel application that we introduced in this chapter as a point of discussion for various issues. This example application is a distributed personnel application, where several possible clients can access information known to the server for different purposes. The client portion of the application allows an end user to manipulate employee information, such as promoting, transferring, and hiring employees. The server portion of the application performs the work that the client requests using whatever data or mechanisms it needs to do the requested work. Although this example shows only one application, the strength of CORBA lies in its ability to support multiple applications.

There are three steps in creating a CORBA-compliant application:

1. Use OMG IDL to define the objects and operations the CORBA application will use.

2.  Develop the client and server sides of the CORBA application using the OMG IDL definitions to generate some of the code.

3.  Deploy the CORBA application.

Parts II, III and IV of this book contain details on each of these steps. However, before you read about these steps, it is important that you have a general understanding of the CORBA architecture, which is described in Chapter 3.

# 3

# An Architectural Overview of CORBA

The CORBA specification describes the components of a CORBA system and what each component should be able to do at a minimum. The specification does not specify the details of how to build a CORBA system product. The specification is more firm on the client side than the server side of the system architecture, particularly with respect to dynamic invocation (discussed in this chapter). This allows each CORBA vendor to support the same system interfaces, but provide differently constructed CORBA systems.

This chapter contains an architectural overview of a CORBA system, including a diagram of the architecture followed by a description of the architecture components and interfaces.

## 3.1 Overview of the CORBA Architecture

Figure 3–1 shows an architectural diagram of a CORBA system. Although this figure shows separate computer systems for the client and server, all components could be on the same computer system. The diagram shows these systems at a snapshot in time. The client and server systems shown do not always have to function as client and server systems. The client system could later function as a server system; likewise the server system could later function as a client system. The purpose of the diagram is to show the interconnection of the components of the CORBA architecture.

Table 3–1 provides a brief description of the components and APIs in the diagram, starting from the top and moving down through the diagram. Following the table, there are sections devoted to key components and interfaces that provide greater detail on them.

For information on the conventions used in this diagram, see the Preface.

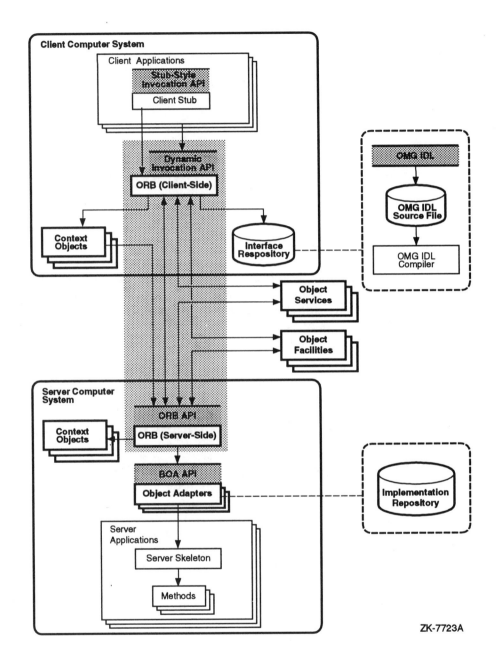

ZK-7723A

**3–2** An Architectural Overview of CORBA

**Table 3–1   CORBA Components and Interfaces**

| Component or Interface | Description |
| --- | --- |
| **Client System** | |
| Client application | The client application uses the CORBA system to invoke operations on some information, data, or application object, such as manipulating employee data for a corporation or reserving airline flights. A server application typically performs these operations. The client application sends a request to a server through either the stub-style invocation API or the dynamic invocation API. |
| Stub-style invocation API | The stub-style invocation API is one of two ways to send a request. This API is a linear programming API that is specific to a particular operation on one kind of object. The stub-style invocation API looks like a function call, and therefore is simpler to use than the dynamic invocation API. CORBA supports only synchronous communication for stub-style invocation. |
| Client stub | The **client stub** provides an interface-specific API and handles all of the CORBA administration functions. A client application can send requests to a server application through a client stub. The OMG IDL compiler generates the client stub. |
| Dynamic invocation API | The dynamic invocation API is one of two ways to send a request. This API is an object-oriented API. The dynamic invocation API uses definitions found in the interface repository to enable the creation and invocation of requests to objects at run time. CORBA supports both synchronous and deferred synchronous communication for dynamic invocation. |
| ORB (client-side) | The Object Request Broker (**ORB**) is a single component, but has some functions specific to the client side and other functions specific to the server side. Figure 3–1 shows this connection using the shading around both the ORB (client-side) and the ORB (server-side) and their interfaces. |

(continued on next page)

Table 3–1 (Cont.)   CORBA Components and Interfaces

| Component or Interface | Description |
| --- | --- |
| **Client System** | |
| ORB (client-side) (Cont.) | The ORB handles invocation requests and the related selection of servers and methods. When an application sends a request to the ORB for an operation on an object, the ORB validates the arguments against the interface and dispatches the request to the server, starting it if necessary. The application can invoke methods synchronously or asynchronously (that is, the application can wait for a response or continue while the server processes the request). The ORB is part of (linked into) the client application itself. |
| Context object | The context object contains information on the client, environment, or a request that is not passed as formal arguments of an operation. The context object is represented as a list of properties and their values. CORBA transmits context object information from the client to the server, and potentially to other servers, to support a set of distributed applications. Application developers can use the context object information for a number of purposes, including influencing server and method selection, user or group profile and preferences (for example, natural language, currency symbols), and general environment information (for example, the default X Window system display device). |
| Interface repository | The **interface repository** stores modules of interface information, such as the interface definitions you code in OMG IDL, and the constants, typedefs, and so on used as part of those definitions. The interface repository includes descriptions of the operations that are valid for a given object and the arguments that are valid for an operation. The interface repository is an integral part of the CORBA system. |
| **Server System** | |
| ORB API | The ORB API enables application developers to access all ORB functions that do not depend on a specific object adapter, such as for creating a list of named values and manipulating object references. |

(continued on next page)

Table 3–1 (Cont.)   CORBA Components and Interfaces

| Component or Interface | Description |
|---|---|
| **Server System** | |
| ORB (server-side) | The ORB is one component, but has some functions specific to the client side and other functions specific to the server side. Figure 3–1 shows this connection using shading around both the ORB (client-side) and the ORB (server-side) and their interfaces. |
| | The ORB is the primary CORBA component on the server side. On the server side, the ORB receives method dispatch requests, unmarshals the arguments, sets up the context state as needed, invokes the method dispatcher in the server skeleton, marshals the output arguments, and completes the invocation. The ORB is part of (linked into) the server application. |
| BOA API | The BOA API enables method developers to access CORBA functions, such as registering implementations, authenticating requests, and handling activation policies. CORBA does not specify a mechanism for binding the application program to the ORB and BOA. The API between the ORB and the BOA and the API between the BOA and the skeletons is vendor-specific. |
| Object adapters | **Object adapters** perform general ORB-related tasks, such as activating objects and implementations and registering server instances. The server skeleton takes these general tasks and ties them to particular implementations and methods in the server. Object adapters are part of (linked into) the server application. The Basic Object Adapter (**BOA**) is the most commonly used object adapter. |
| Server application | The server application uses the server side of the ORB and includes one or more implementations of an object (and their related methods). The methods are the parts of a server application that satisfy a client's request for an operation on a specific object. |

(continued on next page)

**Table 3–1 (Cont.)  CORBA Components and Interfaces**

| Component or Interface | Description |
| --- | --- |
| **Server System** | |
| Server skeleton | The **server skeleton** is a language-specific mapping of OMG IDL operation definitions for an object type (defined by an interface) into methods. The server skeleton provides any code necessary to dispatch a request to the appropriate method. Application developers generate server skeletons from the interface definition. |
| Methods | A method is the code contained in an implementation that actually accomplishes a client's request for an operation on a specific object. A method provides the functions the client application requests. Methods associated with an object can be a single piece of a program's capabilities or a combination of many programs' functions. |
| **Other Components** | |
| OMG IDL | OMG IDL is a definition language that application developers use to define data structures and interface characteristics for objects. Each operation defined on an interface consists of the operation name, arguments, data types, and return values. OMG IDL is not a programming language and cannot be used to generate object or executable code. |
| OMG IDL file | The OMG IDL file is a source file that contains OMG IDL definitions. Application developers use the OMG IDL file to generate source code for the various programming language bindings determined for OMG IDL. |
| OMG IDL compiler | The OMG IDL compiler generates the client stub for the CORBA stub-style invocation API and generates the server skeleton. You might also use the OMG IDL compiler to store OMG IDL definitions in the interface repository depending on your vendor's CORBA system. An OMG IDL compiler is included in most CORBA vendors' systems, but the CORBA specification does not require or describe it. |

(continued on next page)

Table 3–1 (Cont.)  CORBA Components and Interfaces

| Component or Interface | Description |
|---|---|
| **Other Components** | |
| Object Services | Object Services are not a part of CORBA, but they are a complementary part of the object management architecture (OMA) that the OMG defines. The Object Services provide a set of run-time library-like services that support the creation of robust distributed object-oriented applications in the CORBA environment. By using the Object Services, you can make the creation of such applications much easier, just as the use of run-time library routines makes the creation of traditional applications much easier. |
| Object Facilities | Object Facilities are also not a part of CORBA, but a complementary part of OMG's OMA. The Object Facilities are higher-level services and more complex than the Object Services, which are designed to be relatively simple. |
| Implementation repository | The **implementation repository** is a storage place for implementation definitions, such as information about which implementations are installed on a given system. |

The following sections provide more detail on the major CORBA components and interfaces introduced in Table 3–1, their interrelationships, and details on the CORBA specification.

# 3.2 Client Application

The client application invokes requests for operations on objects, which have been defined using OMG IDL. The client application can use the following styles of invocation:

- **Stub-style invocation**

- **Dynamic invocation**

- A mix of both stub-style and dynamic invocation

Each invocation type has different features and is used differently. Stub-style invocation requires the client application to link in client stubs that represent the operations defined for one or more interfaces. Dynamic invocation requires the client application to use operations to access the interface repository and to build a request at run time that it can send. However, whether the client application uses stub-style invocation or dynamic invocation to send the request, the request appears the same on the server side. A server cannot tell whether it was invoked using stubs or dynamically.

Once the client application sends a request and the server application completes it, the client application verifies whether the request completed successfully. If there are problems with a request, the client application can retrieve the exception information and either retry the request or perform some other corrective action as defined in the client application code.

When the request completes successfully, the client application extracts the information it needs to do its job from the arguments to the request. For example, a client operation that retrieves the badge number of an employee would contain an argument that contained that employee's badge number when it completed.

Much of the code in the client application involves calls to the various operations the CORBA **pseudo objects** support, such as calls defined on the context and ORB pseudo objects. Pseudo objects appear the same as other objects in the system. The difference is that the software developer cannot delete or extend pseudo objects because they are part of the system.

For information on the components of a client system and how to put them together, see Chapter 8.

# 3.3 Stub-Style Invocation

The client stub provides definitions and other CORBA vendor-specific information needed to use stub-style invocation in a client application. The client stub maps OMG IDL operation definitions for an object type (defined by an interface definition) into a set of programming language-specific routines that a client application calls to invoke a request.

Client stubs have access to object references and interact with the ORB to perform an invocation of a request. Stubs use proprietary mechanisms optimized for making calls to the ORB. Different ORBs might have different client stubs. Each language mapping provides a programming interface to client stubs for each interface type.

Most CORBA vendors generate client stubs in source code format. However, you should treat client stubs as a component that you only compile and link into your application because some client stub information is private to the CORBA vendor and is subject to change.

# 3.4 Dynamic Invocation

The dynamic invocation API allows run-time creation and invocation of requests to objects. This interface includes the following routines:

- Request routines, such as those used to create a request, add an argument to a request, call the ORB to invoke the appropriate method, or delete a request.

- Deferred synchronous routines, such as those used to initiate an operation, send more than one request in parallel, determine whether a request is completed, and get the next request.

- List routines, such as those used to allocate a list and clear it for initial use and free the list structure and associated memory.

For more information on the tradeoffs in selecting an invocation type and what to do in the client application to use each invocation type, see Chapter 8.

# 3.5 ORB

One of the key features of CORBA is the formal separation of the client from the server, which allows you to develop clients and servers independently as long as they both support the same interface definitions. The ORB is the primary mechanism that CORBA uses to enable the separation of client and server applications. The ORB is defined by its interfaces.

The ORB acts as an intermediary for requests that clients send to servers, so that clients and servers do not need to contain information about each other. The ORB is responsible for all mechanisms required to find the implementation, to prepare the implementation to receive the request, and to communicate the data in the request.

The ORB uses information in the request to determine the best implementation to satisfy the request. This information includes the operation the client is requesting, what type of object the operation is being performed on, and any additional information stored in the context object for this request. Depending on the CORBA vendor, the ORB might also use other, possibly private, information to select an implementation to satisfy a request. This is shown in Figure 3–2.

**Figure 3–2  The ORB Selecting an Implementation to Perform a Request**

```
┌─────────────────────┐   Sends request
│  Client Application │   to the ORB
└─────────────────────┘
           │
           ▼
┌──────────┐            ORB selects the implementation
│   ORB    │            to perform the request and sends
└──────────┘            the request to that implementation
     │
     │   ┌────────────────────────────────────┐
     │   │  Server A                          │
     │   │   ┌──────────────────────────┐     │
     │   │   │  Implementation A.1      │     │
     │   │   └──────────────────────────┘     │
     │   │   ┌──────────────────────────┐     │
     └──────▶│  Implementation A.2      │     │
         │   └──────────────────────────┘     │
         └────────────────────────────────────┘

         ┌────────────────────────────────────┐
         │  Server B                          │
         │   ┌──────────────────────────┐     │
         │   │  Implementation A.1      │     │
         │   └──────────────────────────┘     │
         └────────────────────────────────────┘
```

ZK-7724A

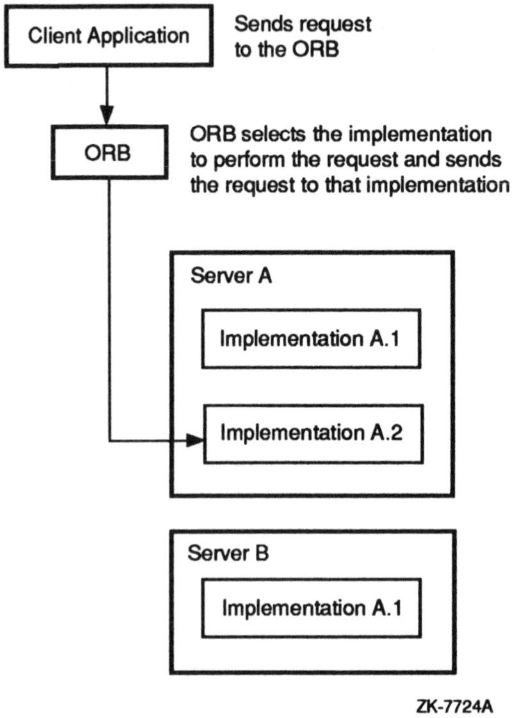

In addition to selecting the implementation to perform a request, the ORB also validates each request and its arguments and can provide authentication or authorization information. For example, the ORB checks that the object specified in the request is valid for the operation being requested. The ORB also searches the implementation repository to determine whether the ORB knows about an implementation that can service the client request.

The ORB is also a pseudo object that has operations defined on it that both client and server application developers can use. For example, a client application developer can use the CORBA_ORB_create_list operation to create a list of named values for the dynamic invocation of a request, or a server application developer can use the CORBA_ORB_obj_to_string operation to convert a CORBA object reference into a string so CORBA can store it in a file rather than in memory.

Although Figure 3–1 shows the ORB on the client side as well as the server side, there is really one ORB with code that addresses both the client and server sides. With Version 2.0 and later versions, it will be possible for a CORBA system to have multiple ORBs. Multiple ORBs could have different representations for object references and different invocation styles. If a client application has access to two object references managed by different ORBs, the ORBs rather than the client applications must distinguish their object references.

# 3.6 Context Objects

The context objects contain information on the client, environment, or circumstances of a request that is not passed as an argument to an operation. The application developer uses operations defined on the ContextObject interface to create and manipulate context objects. The context object stores its information as a list of properties, which consist of an identifier and an associated string value. For example, display could be a context object identifier that indicates the display device the end user is currently using, and Xwindows or PC could be the string value associated with the display identifier.

Context objects can be temporary (in memory) or persistent (on disk) and can have an associated scope. Thus, application developers can use this scope to group different levels of attributes on a given platform and provide the desired default and override behavior for these attributes. For instance, application developers can represent the concept of user, work group, and system-level attributes with context objects.

Both the client application and the ORB can read from or write to the context object. The client application uses the context object to describe the preferred environment for the request. For example, context object properties can represent a portion of the client's or application's environment meant to become part of, or propagated to, the server's environment. Particular operation definitions can specify context properties for the operation.

The ORB can write to the context object to add its preferences for the request to those of the client application. Because the context object is passed as an implicit argument, the ORB can use information in the context object to select an implementation, by influencing method behavior, server location, or activation policy.

CORBA specifies that the context object information is optional, so the ORB does not depend on that information being supplied. However, requests might contain an argument that references the context object.

The ORB will look for a context object only if both of the following are true:

- There is a context clause in OMG IDL defining the operation.

- The client application is using the dynamic invocation interface, which requires the use of the context object, even if the context object is NULL.

# 3.7 Interface Repository

The interface repository contains descriptions of the interfaces of applications and data objects that exist in the network. The primary function of the interface repository is to provide information for dynamically invoked requests. The client application uses the interface repository during dynamic invocation to get the signature of the operation that is being requested, including any user-defined types. A **signature** is a general programming term for the arguments associated with a routine or operation. In CORBA, the signature for an operation includes the arguments that are part of that specific operation, their data types, direction, and the return type.

The interface repository contains the same kind of invocation information that an implementation of CORBA might store in its client stubs for stub-style invocation. The client application accesses the interface repository as part of the dynamic invocation process using the operations that CORBA defines for this purpose, such as CORBA_InterfaceDef_describe_interface.

Application developers can also use the interface repository as follows:

- To manage the installation and distribution of interface definitions

  By storing interface definitions in the interface repository, developers can update those definitions by updating only the definition in the repository, rather than every OMG IDL file that uses it. Also, if an interface definition includes a number of inherited or referenced definitions (such as interfaces, operations, or data type definitions), developers can make these inherited files available for use when generating server skeletons or client stubs by storing them in the interface repository instead of requiring the OMG IDL files to be distributed.

- As a development tool if the CORBA vendor provides a browser

  Such a browser could allow developers to scan the repository and find interface definitions to reuse and add to their own OMG IDL file, to use in writing their client application, or to use in writing an implementation that supports that interface definition for a server application.

Although CORBA defines how to read information from the interface repository, it does not specify how to construct or load the repository. CORBA leaves these details to the CORBA vendors. Therefore, interface repositories from different CORBA vendors will likely have different:

- Features, such as versioning, concurrency, and integrity checking.

- Flexibility and distribution capabilities, such as a single centralized repository for all applications and users of the CORBA system, or an interface repository for each computer or each user, or some combination of these options.

- Tools to support the interface repository, such as a repository browser.

The features and tools each vendor provides for using the interface repository might be important to you in selecting a CORBA vendor.

# 3.8 OMG IDL

OMG IDL is a definition language and not a programming language. That is, you can use OMG IDL to define interfaces and data structures. The OMG has defined various programming language bindings for OMG IDL. You can generate source code for those languages from the OMG IDL source file or possibly directly from the interface repository. Typically, CORBA vendors generate language bindings in C, C++, and Smalltalk because these are the only language bindings the OMG has currently specified for OMG IDL.

You can use OMG IDL to define types of objects by defining their interfaces. The body of an interface declares the constants exported, declaration type, exceptions, attributes, and operations. Operation definitions include the operation name, type of data returned, types of all arguments, valid exceptions returned, and contextual information that could affect method dispatch.

# 3.9 OMG IDL File and Compiler

An OMG IDL file describes the data structures, operations, and objects that the client can request and that an implementation on a server must provide to support that client. CORBA vendors generate programming language-specific files from OMG IDL files, which have been input into one or both of the following components:

- OMG IDL compiler

  To generate programming language-specific files from an OMG IDL compiler, developers input the OMG IDL source file into the compiler and the compiler generates one or more of these files based on the switches the developer specifies to the compiler. An OMG IDL compiler is a part of most

CORBA vendors' systems because it tends to be very useful to CORBA application developers, but it is not required by the CORBA specification.

- Interface repository

  To generate programming language-specific files from an interface repository, developers must load the OMG IDL file into the interface repository in some way and then generate one or more programming language-specific files from the interface repository. The exact procedure for loading the OMG IDL file or generating these files will vary among CORBA vendors.

The following are the programming language-specific files that can be generated from the information in the OMG IDL file:

- Client stub files

  The client application uses client stub files during the stub-style invocation of a request. A client stub maps OMG IDL operation definitions for an object type (that is described by an interface definition) into routines, one routine for each operation that is part of the interface. These client stubs typically are generated in source code format and compiled and linked into the client application.

- Header files

  Both client and server applications use header files to define data types, such as structures and constants, that both the client and the server application use. These header files typically are included into the client and the server application source code.

- Server skeleton files

  The server application uses the server skeleton files to map client operations to methods in the implementation on the server. These skeletons typically are generated in source code format and are compiled and linked into the server application.

Figure 3–3 shows the files that can be generated from the interface definitions in an OMG IDL file. In this example, the interface definitions in the file CORP.IDL are used to generate a client stub file, CORP_cstub.c, a header file, CORP.h, and a server skeleton, CORP_sskel.c. These files are generated from either an interface repository after the interface definitions have been loaded into the repository or from an OMG IDL compiler.

**Figure 3–3  Client and Server Files Generated from an OMG IDL File**

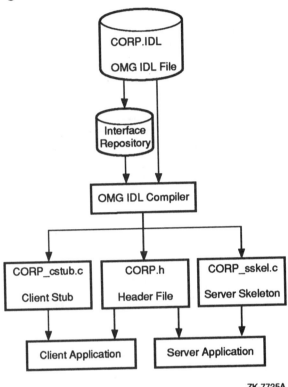

ZK-7725A

## 3.10 Server Application

A server application contains one or more implementations, which are the parts of a server that accomplish a client's request for operations on a specific object. When a client sends a request to the ORB, the ORB selects an implementation to satisfy that request and uses the BOA to direct the request to that implementation. The BOA uses the server skeletons to call the methods within the implementation.

The server application that the developer creates needs to contain several pieces of code to do the following:

- Initialize the server application.

- Handle service requests.

- Shut down the server application.

Figure 3–4 shows this basic structure of a server application.

**Figure 3–4  Basic Structure of a Server Application**

ZK-7726A

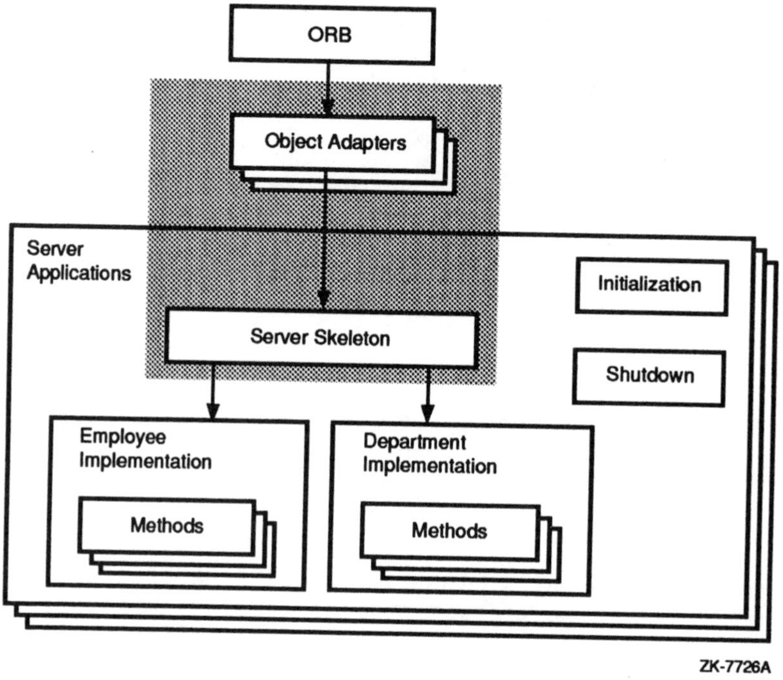

Much of the code for a server application involves calls to the various operations that the CORBA pseudo objects support, such as calls defined on the BOA, context, and ORB pseudo objects. For more information on the components of a server application and how to put them together, see Chapter 9.

## 3.11 Object Adapters

An object adapter is the primary mechanism for managing object references and implementations on the server. The role of the object adapter is to provide ORB services to the implementation. Given the variety of services an ORB can potentially be asked to handle, CORBA provides for the possibility of multiple object adapters, each tailored to work effectively with different groups of objects. However, CORBA requires only one object adapter, the BOA, which provides the common services.

An object adapter can do the following:

- Provide a binding between an object's interface and a server's implementation of the object.

- Generate and interpret object references and map the object references to implementations.

- Activate and deactivate objects and implementations.

- Register implementations.

- Implicitly invoke implementation methods through the skeleton.

## 3.11.1 Basic Object Adapter

CORBA has designed the Basic Object Adapter (BOA) to be the most commonly used object adapter. All CORBA vendors must supply a BOA as part of their systems.

Some CORBA vendors might provide additional specialized object adapters, such as library object adapters or object-oriented database adapters. However, those object adapters and how they function will vary among vendors. In this section, we will focus on the BOA because it is the only object adapter that CORBA defines, and it is likely that more specialized vendor-specific object adapters will be very similar to the BOA.

In most CORBA systems, the ORB passes request arguments and control to the BOA, which handles the process of selecting and activating an implementation and returns results to the ORB. The BOA connects the ORB to the methods in the implementation by using server skeletons (these are the server skeletons that were generated from the interface definitions). These server skeletons contain routines that map calls from the BOA to the methods in a particular implementation that supports the requested operation. Figure 3–5 illustrates this mapping, where CORBA sends the request for the dismiss operation from the client application through the BOA and server skeletons to the Emp_dismiss method in the employee implementation in the server application. The dashed line indicates the data flow.

## 3.11.2 BOA Operations

In addition to being the connecting point between the ORB and the server skeletons, the BOA is also a pseudo object that has operations defined on it that server application developers can use (the client application developer does not need these operations). The C binding for these operations all have the prefix CORBA_BOA_, which indicates that these operations are defined on the BOA object. For example, developers can use the CORBA_BOA_create operation to create an object reference for a new instance of an object, and the CORBA_BOA_set_exception operation to signal an exception if there is a problem performing the requested operation.

**Figure 3–5  The BOA Connecting the ORB to the Implementation Methods**

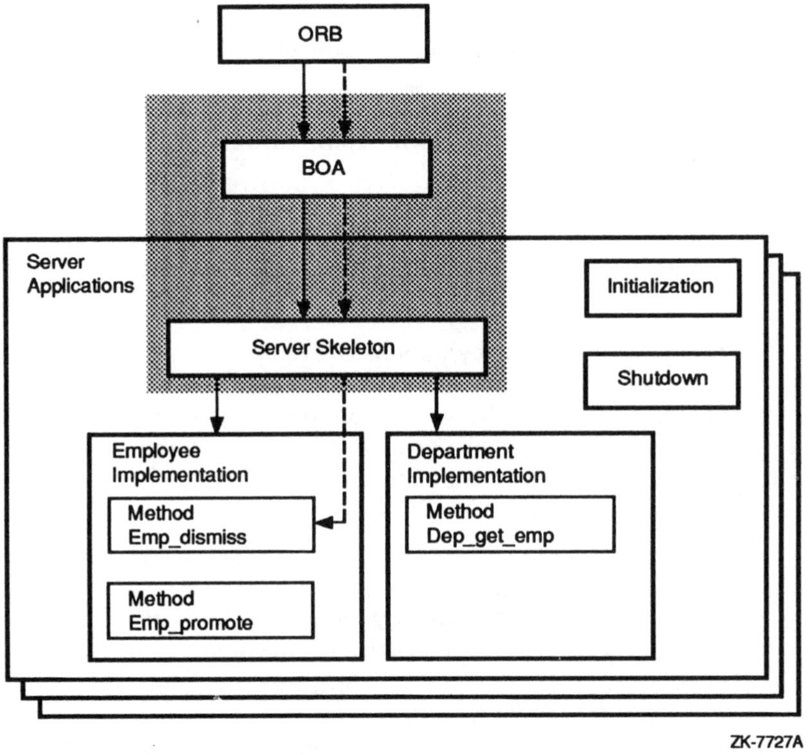

ZK-7727A

The BOA can activate an implementation and can also deactivate it, depending on how the CORBA vendor handles implementation deactivation. **Activation** prepares an object to execute operations, such as copying stored data into the implementation's memory to allow execution of methods on the stored data. **Deactivation** releases an implementation, so that it can no longer accept requests. The BOA also provides a group of operations that allow the server application developer to manage objects, object references, and implementations on the server.

Although CORBA spells out the minimum set of operations and capabilities that a BOA must provide, it does not describe how to accomplish many of them. Information that will vary among CORBA vendors includes how the BOA is associated with the ORB, the server, or the methods in the implementations on the server (through the server skeletons). For example, the BOA might be associated through some look-up mechanism, such as a name service or a registry, or through some other means.

## 3.12 Server Skeletons

Server skeletons provide the connection between the BOA and the methods that accomplish each operation on an object. Skeletons contain information necessary to map an operation on an object to the appropriate implementation and method. Skeletons are generated from OMG IDL definitions and are specific to a particular interface and object adapter.

When the ORB receives a request, it contacts the BOA through a mechanism that is private to the vendor. Once the BOA has selected the appropriate implementation, it notifies the server by calling routines contained in the server skeleton. The skeleton links the BOA to the appropriate implementation and method for the request.

## 3.13 The Implementation Repository

The implementation repository contains information that allows the ORB to locate and activate implementations of objects. CORBA uses the implementation repository to associate object references with implementations, just as it uses the interface repository to associate object references with their interfaces. The BOA expects information describing implementations to be stored in an implementation repository. The implementation repository stores these implementation definitions in ImplementationDef pseudo objects.

Most of the information in an implementation repository is specific to a vendor's ORB or operating environment. Developers and administrators can use operations on the implementation repository to install implementations and control policies related to the activation and execution of implementations.

The CORBA specification does not say much more about the implementation repository. Therefore, CORBA vendors will determine what operations to use to access the repository, how to construct it, and any capabilities it has beyond those already described. For example, the implementation repository might contain additional information for debugging server applications or for server administration. You might also be able to use the implementation repository as an implementation browser in a CORBA development environment.

## 3.14 What's Next

The following chapter is the beginning of Part II, Designing a CORBA Application. This part is intended for the application designer who will determine the overall design of a particular CORBA application in an enterprise. Part III then discusses how to develop a CORBA application, which includes generating executable code. The information we have provided in

Chapters 1, 2, and 3 should give you the background for an understanding of the design and development issues in the rest of the book.

# Part II
## For the Application Designer: Designing a CORBA Application Framework

Part II shows the application designer how to design an application or application framework to run in a CORBA environment. Part II includes the following chapters:

- Chapter 4 describes how to design a CORBA application or application framework.

- Chapter 5 describes how to refine your design model to be efficient and extensible.

- Chapter 6 describes some considerations in distributing your design.

- Chapter 7 contains general guidelines on coding your object model in OMG IDL.

# 4

# Designing a CORBA Application

There are many decisions you need to make in designing an object-oriented application. This chapter presents an overview of the specific design decisions you need to make when building a CORBA application. It includes a description of application frameworks and details a four-step process for designing a CORBA application or framework.

## 4.1 Application Frameworks

When designing an application for a CORBA distributed object system, it is useful to think in terms of application frameworks. An **application framework** is a collection of interacting applications and other software components that are used together for some specific purpose, such as creating software or managing a bank's assets. For example, a framework for software development could include a source code editor, a compiler, a debugger, a source code management system, and a testing application. Application frameworks can simplify complex processes, such as those used for computer-aided software engineering (CASE) or those used for purchasing/inventory control.

The infrastructure of an application framework often includes a collection of software components that developers use to build applications for the problem the framework solves. Application frameworks can also contain specialized APIs, services, and tools, thus reducing the knowledge an end user or developer needs to have to accomplish a specific task. Frameworks also describe how tools are used together.

The Distributed Computing Environment (DCE) is an example of a framework. DCE consists of numerous applications, such as the RPC runtime library, authentication services, and directory services, that work together in the DCE framework. DCE provides the APIs that enable clients to use the DCE application components as needed in a DCE environment or framework.

### 4.1.1 Using Frameworks

The idea of using frameworks has been around for some time and is not a new idea with the CORBA architecture. The problem with creating frameworks, though, is that the framework must integrate new and existing applications, typically each of which has a different API for accessing its capabilities. The CORBA architecture simplifies the creation of frameworks because it provides a consistent object-oriented paradigm that is used by all applications in the framework.

The CORBA system expresses the capabilities that an application can provide to other applications as one or more sets of operations defined on various objects. This means that the CORBA system will request and perform any action in a CORBA framework as an operation on an object.

The CORBA architecture also allows the applications in your framework to be insulated from whether those applications are all running on the same system. In a CORBA system, a client and server have no direct knowledge of each other, and therefore, no knowledge of whether they are both running on the same system or are distributed across a network. This insulation simplifies application development because the application does not have to contain code that handles whether it is communicating with a local or remote application. The insulation of clients from servers in a CORBA system also allows you to add application clients and servers to an existing framework without having to update, recompile, and redeploy all the parts of that framework.

Businesses today are looking to frameworks to solve problems of handling increasingly complicated tasks that require integration of multiple new and legacy applications.

### 4.1.2 Designing Frameworks

Frameworks can be open or closed or a combination of both types. An **open framework** is a framework that allows you to remove and replace software components easily in a "plug-and-play" fashion. A **closed framework** does not have this flexibility, but it can nevertheless be an efficient solution to a problem. Most frameworks are not completely open or completely closed, but fall somewhere in between.

Generally, it is best to design a framework to be as open as possible, even if you have no plans to add to or change the components in the framework. Requirements can unexpectedly change; an open framework enables you to respond to the changes more quickly.

## 4.2 Designing a Distributed Application as a Framework

The CORBA distributed object system can handle both distributed and nondistributed applications or frameworks. Because it is most likely that your applications will be distributed, this section discusses some of the design issues to consider for distributed applications.

When designing distributed software, there are many issues to consider in addition to building the software and installing its parts. For example, with distributed software, you might need to make decisions on one or more of the following topics:

- What types of network transports are required to communicate between the applications of your framework?

  You need to ensure that your ORB can use the necessary network transports. There are a variety of network transports to consider at varying levels, such as programming paradigms (AppleTalk and DCE RPC), communication protocols (DECnet, DECnet/OSI, IBM 2780/3780, Novell IPX/SPX, SNA, TCP/IP, and X.25), communications mediums (Ethernet and serial line), and whether the communications is connected or disconnected (mobile computing). Different types of applications function over different types of network transports. It is important to plan for the types of network transports that you will need in your framework.

- What style of communication is required in your framework?

  The CORBA architecture defines three communication styles: synchronous, asynchronous (or deferred synchronous in CORBA terms), and one-way. Different styles might be better suited for different frameworks.

  For example, there are times when synchronous communication between a client and server is the best choice, such as when a client request results in the server performing short time-critical operations such as computing a monthly mortgage payment.

  On the other hand, asynchronous communication is the best choice when a client cannot wait for a response to the request before issuing the next request. For example, if a client requests a server to format and print several large documents, it is probably best to send those requests asynchronously so the client can continue to do other work while the server formats and prints the documents.

  And in other cases, one-way communication might be the best choice when the client does not need confirmation that a task is completed, such as when logging events, notifying applications that an event occurred, or when used in a distributed system management tool.

  For more information on these communication styles, see Chapter 8.

- What types of hardware and software platforms will the software run on?

  Computer platforms (pairs of computer hardware and operating systems) come in many forms. Because of the differences among platforms, software created to run on one platform usually will not run on another platform without expensive and time-consuming modifications. While you might avoid this problem by standardizing all software on a single platform, this is usually not practical or cost-effective.

- How can your framework minimize the use of system resources?

  In a nondistributed environment, you can call a routine ten times within the same process and those calls will not consume a significant amount of system resources. However, if you make those same ten calls in a distributed environment to another process across the network, they might consume a significant portion of system resources (in particular, network resources, such as sockets, communication channels, and logical links).

- What other aspects must you consider with remote applications?

  There are other considerations for remote applications. For example, you need to plan what should happen if a client invokes a request and the server is not available, is unknown, or the client does not have access to it. You also need to plan for situations where the client invokes a request that fails for some reason other than network problems.

Whether you are designing a fairly simple distributed application or a complex framework to use with a CORBA system, it is a good idea to design them as a framework, because by doing so you build in the ability to modify and extend the application easily. For example, the personnel application introduced in the following section has three types of entities: employees, departments, and personnel. By designing this application as a framework, you can easily add other entities, such as managers or budgets, because the application provides an existing infrastructure to support them.

## 4.3 Designing the Model

The initial stages of the CORBA design process involve designing a model of the application functions. **Modeling** is a design technique used in developing architecture, simulations, and in this case, computer systems. There are four steps to this design process as follows:

1. Identify the problems to be solved

2. Create an abstract model that solves the problem

3. Create an object model that solves the problem

4. Represent the model in OMG IDL code

The following section introduces an example that we use in this book to show how to design, develop, and deploy a CORBA application framework. Details on the four-step design process follow the example.

## 4.3.1 Example Framework

To illustrate the issues involved in designing a distributed object-oriented application, we will use an example company that is reorganizing and consolidating several organizations into one organization called Corporate Services. Each organization that the company is moving into Corporate Services has previous applications that they purchased or developed for their own particular needs. The company needs to develop a new personnel application for the Corporate Services framework that blends the needs of all organizations into one application.

The existing department-specific personnel applications access and store their information in different ways and run on different hardware and software. For example, several different applications currently handle information about employees and store that information separately. Whenever an employee joins or leaves the company, someone in personnel must access and update each application.

As part of the Corporate Services consolidation, the information services manager wants to integrate all the software applications that the various departments use. The information services manager has purchased a CORBA system to use to integrate the applications into a single, distributed, integrated framework. The company has future plans to use this framework as a template for creating other frameworks in other parts of the company, such as Sales or Engineering.

Throughout this book, we will be designing, developing, and deploying the Corporate Services framework. We will include fragments of OMG IDL and C code to illustrate various points. Appendix A contains the complete listing of these code examples in OMG IDL and C and also in C++.

## 4.3.2 Step 1: Identify the Problems to Be Solved

The first step in designing an application or framework is to gather the requirements. One way to do this is to ask the following questions:

- What problems do you want this application to solve?

  For example, the Corporate Services personnel application addresses problems of data sharing, use of existing resources, and extensibility.

The goals of the personnel application are:

— To share all common data with the other software components in the framework.

— To distribute the software across the various company hardware and software platforms to make the best use of existing resources.

— To enable easy extensibility so the software can support new capabilities as needed.

• What business environment must the personnel application manage?

For example, our personnel application needs to be able to manage all employee information for the corporation. End users of the application need to be able to do the following tasks:

— Hire employees into the company

— Promote employees within the company

— Transfer employees between departments

— Dismiss an employee from the company

— Update an employee's personnel information

• Do I need to design some or all of my data to be secure?

Whether you need a security scheme for your data can greatly affect how you design the data and access to the data. You may want to restrict certain end users or certain other objects or services from using a particular set of data. For example, you may want only the direct manager of an employee to be able to retrieve that employee's salary information.

Some CORBA vendors supply security capabilities that you can use with your application or framework for authorization and authentication. You may choose to use these capabilities, create your own capabilities, or use them both together to make the security arrangements that your application or framework requires. We'll talk more about security in Part III.

• Do I need to design some or all of my data to be extensible?

When you are designing your application or framework, you know that certain data will probably never change and other data will be changed at some point, such as:

— The badge number of an employee is unlikely to change.

There will always be a need to handle a particular badge number and badge numbers will always fall in a fairly small range. Even if your company grows to several million employees, your badge numbers will still be easily contained in a relatively small amount of memory.

- A company database that contains information about all funded projects is very likely to change.

  For example, for space considerations, you might initially limit the text information for the project description to only 512 characters. But at the same time, you anticipate the need to extend the description in the future to handle greater amounts of text and possibly multimedia as well. Your design needs to allow for this potential change.

If you expect to extend certain kinds of data, you can use some special data-related objects and operations to enable extensibility. For example, in our product database, we know we want to extend the description object in the future. We also have other information objects in other parts of our system that we will want to extend in the same way. Therefore, we decide to create a data_stream object for all implementations of these extensible information objects to use. The data_stream object handles data as a stream of some number of bytes rather than as an absolute type, such as a null-terminated string containing 5 characters. The data_stream object can handle any kind and amount of data because it treats any data as an endless stream of bytes. The data in the bytes can be ASCII text or multimedia information. Some of the operations we have defined on the data_stream object are open, close, read, write, and so on.

Designing certain information objects to use the same data_stream object and operations in their implementations increases the reliability and modularity of the application and avoids writing a lot of code. In addition, developers can add operations to the data_stream object in a single interface and all implementations that use the data_stream object can benefit from the new operations. This reuse of objects is one of the great benefits of using object-oriented systems like CORBA.

## 4.3.3 Step 2: Create an Abstract Model

The second step in designing an application or framework is to create an abstract model of how the application will solve the requirements you identified in step 1. An **abstract model** describes the activities that end users might need to perform (hiring, promoting, transferring) and the entities involved (managers and departments). Creating an abstract model of an application typically enables you to improve the design and construction of your software and to make the software easier to maintain, extend, and reuse.

To create this abstract model, you use the task descriptions that you created in step 1 to identify the following:

- Activities to be modeled—for example, promoting a person from one job to another job.

- Entities involved in these activities—for example, the employee who is being promoted.

- Constraints upon the entities or the activities—for example, the need for some sort of approval process for a promotion.

Using our example personnel application, we can model how the software will handle employee information. Table 4–1 shows how to map the task descriptions from step 1 to the activities, entities, and constraints in the application.

**Table 4–1  Abstract Model of the Personnel Application**

| Task Description | Activity | Entities Involved | Potential Constraints |
|---|---|---|---|
| Hiring employees into the company | Hire employee | Personnel | Need management approval |
| Promoting employees within the company | Promote employee | Employee | Need management approval |
| Transferring employees between departments | Transfer employee | Employee and Department | Need management approval |
| Dismissing an employee from the company | Dismiss employee | Employee | Need management approval |
| Updating an employee's personnel information | Update employee | Employee | |

If you have described the requirements clearly, it is not too difficult to identify the activities and entities. In most cases, the verbs in your task descriptions are the activities and the nouns are the entities.

## 4.3.4 Step 3: Create an Object Model

The third step in designing an application or framework is to convert the abstract model to an object model for use with a CORBA system. An object model expresses the functions of an application in object-oriented terms, such as objects, attributes, operations, and the relationships between them. The object model is particularly helpful for understanding how the objects and operations will interact in a distributed environment.

To translate an abstract model into an object model, you need to:

1. List all activities as operations.

2. List all entities as objects.

3. Associate all operations with their respective objects. For example, the promote operation manipulates the employee object, which indicates that the employee is being promoted, not that the employee is doing the promoting. Table 4–2 shows the result of a first attempt to translate the abstract model of the personnel application into objects and operations.

**Table 4–2   Translating Activities and Entities Into Objects and Operations**

| Activity | Entity Involved | Operation | Object |
|----------|-----------------|-----------|--------|
| Hire employee | Personnel | Hire | Personnel |
| Promote employee | Employee | Promote | Employee |
| Transfer employee | Employee and Department | Transfer | Employee |
| Dismiss employee | Employee | Dismiss | Employee |
| Update employee information | Employee | Update | Employee |

4. Group the objects and related operations

   For example, Table 4–3 shows a possible grouping of the objects and related operations in the personnel application.

Table 4–3  Objects and Operations in the Personnel Application

| Object | Operation Defined on Object |
| --- | --- |
| Personnel | Hire |
| Employee | Promote<br>Dismiss<br>Update<br>Transfer |
| Department | |

All the operations manipulate the personnel object or the employee object. The employee is transferred, not the department. If there were a larger scope of activities and entities that the personnel application used, it is possible that a department object would have one or more operations defined on it.

5. Refine the object model.

To ensure that your CORBA application or framework runs as efficiently as possible and is easily extensible, you need to look at a number of things that will help you refine your model to be the best possible model.

For example, in our personnel application it is not clear whether the application needs all of these objects and operations and whether we have associated the right operations with the right objects. Refining the object model will help make these decisions.

Important guidelines for refining the object model are:

- Use a real-world model
- Make operations generic for multiple application use
- Determine the most efficient way to create objects
- Use interface inheritance
- Use operations and attributes effectively

For more information on using these guidelines to refine your object model, see Chapter 5.

### 4.3.5 Step 4: Represent the Object Model in OMG IDL Code

The fourth step in designing an application or framework is to describe the design of your framework to the CORBA system by representing it in OMG IDL code.

A CORBA interface definition, coded in OMG IDL, defines the characteristics and behavior of a kind of object, including the operations that can be performed on the object. You use OMG IDL to identify the interfaces (objects and associated operations) that clients will use to request that work be done and the interfaces that servers will support to do the work. The OMG IDL definitions also make it possible to map CORBA objects into particular programming languages or object systems, such as C or C++.

As you create your OMG IDL descriptions, you will probably find it to be an iterative process like most programming. You will change your design to match concepts in your OMG IDL, and you will change your OMG IDL to match concepts in your design.

Chapter 7 provides more information on coding your model in OMG IDL, including information on whether to use simple or complex types for object attributes and how to use exceptions with your operations and object attributes.

## 4.4 Contrasting an Object-Oriented with a Data-Centered Design Model

This section highlights the advantages of an object-oriented model for a CORBA application over a more traditional data-centered design model.

If we were to use a traditional data-centered approach for the personnel application in this chapter, we might have the client application explicitly create, modify, and delete employee records. The client application might use a relational database and relational database statements for promoting new employees rather than using object-oriented promote operations on personnel objects. Examples of such relational database statements are:

```
insert into Employees (last_name, first_name, ... ) ...
insert into Department (dept_id, employee_id, ... ) ...
```

When designing this distributed application for a CORBA system, we could have operations that model the data-centered approach and that closely approximate these database operations, such as insert_record operations on employee_relation objects. However, there are several inherent problems with such a data-centered approach in a CORBA system.

The major problems with a data-centered approach are:

- Data-centered operations are limited to one task on data.

  For example, the data-centered `insert_record` operation lets the client insert only the employee name. An object-oriented model enables an operation to perform many tasks at once, such as entering the employee name, badge number, department name, and manager. This supports the use of a real-world model and insulation of operations from specific implementations of those operations.

- Data-centered client applications need more extensive information, making code changes more difficult.

  For example, in a data-centered approach to our personnel application, the client applications would require extensive information about the entire hiring and promotion process. Clients would need to know which records in which relations (and which databases) to update. And, if the hiring and promotion process changes, you would have to recode and redeploy all your client applications.

- Data-centered client applications require more steps to perform a task, such as promoting an employee.

  Having unnecessary steps in a distributed application is inefficient and costly, especially if these operations require remote calls over the network.

- Data-centered approaches introduce ambiguity and potential coding problems at a later time.

  For example, with the personnel application model, the promote operation is potentially ambiguous. That is, it is not clear whether the application performing the promote operation is requesting that the employee be promoted or whether it is stating that the employee has already been promoted and is issuing a notification of the approved decision.

  When designing the initial data-centered model, you might not formally differentiate the requester from the approver, in which case you would not initially see any problems with the design. However, if the process to promote employees changes to require an approval cycle, you will need to modify your client applications to incorporate the approval. Or, you might need to determine which end users are using each application to determine which applications to modify.

## 4.5 For More Information

The process of designing an object-oriented application or framework is a
substantial undertaking. There are many books devoted to this subject, which
outline various approaches and considerations. The design steps presented
in this chapter are one such approach. For more information about other
approaches and design tips for object-oriented applications or frameworks, see
the preface for a listing of related object-oriented analysis and design books.

# 5

# Refining Your Object Model

Refining your CORBA object model ensures that your CORBA application or framework will run as efficiently as possible and is easily extensible. You want to refine your model to be the best possible model before you begin coding. In all software, but especially in distributed object-oriented software such as CORBA, it is better to spend a little extra time on the design, so as to avoid recoding later on.

This chapter contains information on refining your model, including more detail on the following guidelines introduced in the previous chapter:

- Use a real-world model
- Make operations generic for multiple application use
- Determine the most efficient way to create objects
- Use interface inheritance
- Use operations and attributes effectively

## 5.1 Using a Real-World Model

The first guideline in refining your object model is to base your design on a real-world model. That is, you should select operations and objects that are part of the real nonsoftware world. For example, an employee is something that is real and the process of promoting an employee is something that is part of the real world. By contrast, an employee data structure or a `promote_employee` routine are found only in software.

By using a real-world model for your framework, you:

- Make the framework easier for yourself and others to understand
- Avoid creating complex or artificial constructs to make part of the model work
- Avoid placing unnecessary limits on the framework

- Make it easier to validate and extend the framework

- Can test whether objects or operations are set up realistically and efficiently

For example, we showed in the previous chapter that having promote and dismiss operations available on an employee object makes sense in the real world. Suppose we now need to extend our model to include the ability to transfer employees. Because we understand how promoting and dismissing works as an operation on an employee object, we can easily extend that object to include the transfer operation.

## 5.2 Making Operations Generic

When you are selecting the operations that the objects in your framework will use, you should make sure that the operations are not specific to one implementation. Your operations should be generic enough to use multiple implementations. For example, suppose your design specifies that the Edit operation invoke the vi editor only. A glance at the real world suggests that Emacs is also used in the computing environment, and other text editors not used currently might eventually need to be made available. Thus, you should revise your Edit operation design to call Emacs as well as vi and to allow for the addition of other editors in the future.

The more possible implementations you can take under consideration for your operation, the better the chance that your operation is well insulated from how it will be implemented. If you can think of only one possible implementation for an operation, you should take another look at the operation and make sure it is not too specific to an implementation. You might need to think about modeling that operation more abstractly.

For example, a good abstract operation and object would be an update operation on an employee object. You could handle this type of operation in several different ways. A poor example would be having a change_field operation on an employee_record object. This example locks you into an implementation that uses records and fields.

Designing operations in this fashion also supports an important programming practice known as **information hiding**. Information hiding is a technique for providing a module of code with only the information it needs to do its job. In structured programming, developers use information hiding to make the variables that a routine uses local to that routine rather than making them available globally throughout the module or program.

# 5.3 Determining How to Create Objects

Object creation is one of the thorniest design problems in an object-oriented system. How do you obtain an object on which to perform an operation when that object does not yet exist? When determining how to create objects, you must give the client application neither too much nor too little information about the object creation process. To make it easier to understand this problem, let's examine how it occurs and is resolved in the design of the personnel application.

### First Try: Putting the Hire Operation on the Employee Object

One might possibly attempt to place the hire operation on the employee object because, in the real world, the hiring process brings a job candidate into the company as an employee. However, the hire operation is a special case because it actually creates an instance of the employee object to represent the individual being hired. Basically, the problem was how to have an employee hire themselves before they exist as an employee.

The first attempt to solve the object creation problem is to place the hire operation on the employee object and use an external tool to create the employee object when an end user invokes the hire operation.

This approach provides no information about object creation to the client application; the process is completely hidden. However, it is hidden so well that it is now difficult to create objects because the application must always use this outside tool. The application cannot create objects as a result of an operation.

Using an object creation tool is fine on initial startup of a CORBA system, but using it to create all objects in a system could become cumbersome.

### Second Try: Putting the Hire Operation on the Manager Object

A second attempt to solve the object creation problem places the hire operation on the future manager of the employee. This approach reflects real-world practices, wherein managers decide which employees to hire. Unfortunately, the client application now needs to find both the department the employee is being hired into and the manager of that department to perform the hire operation.

Although object creation is now easier than in our first attempt, the client application now requires more information than it should about how the hiring process works. If this hiring process changes, for example, by requiring an additional manager to be involved, the server methods that support the hiring process will have to be changed, as will any client applications that might request that operation, such changes in process should be invisible to the client application.

Placing the hire operation on the manager object causes the need for all the additional information. Managers approve and initiate the hiring of employees, but the personnel representative actually does the hiring.

### Getting It Right: Putting the Hire Operation on the Personnel Object

Because the personnel department tends to control all information on hiring, a more accurate reflection of the real world in the model is to make the personnel object the sole owner of information about the hire operation. Only the personnel object really needs information about what managers need to be contacted, whether or not an approval process is needed, and if so, which approval process, and so on.

By placing the hire operation on the personnel object, we have the best solution to the object creation problem. The client application has enough information about the hiring process. It needs to know only to use the hire operation on a personnel object to hire an employee; it does not need information about departments or managers for this employee. If the hiring process changes, you must change only the personnel object because the hiring process is encapsulated in the personnel object; the employee and manager objects are not affected.

## 5.4 Using Interface Inheritance

One of the major benefits of CORBA is that you can take advantage of interface inheritance, which allows you to pass along characteristics of one interface to another. Not all object-oriented systems support interface inheritance. The CORBA designers, however, felt it was important for application designers and developers to have this capability. In CORBA, interfaces inherit everything that is defined as part of the interface from which they are inheriting.

It is important not to confuse interface inheritance with the idea of containment. Containment is the encapsulation of an entity within another entity; for example, a field within a record or a routine within a module. Interface inheritance passes on the characteristics from one interface to another; for example, a manager interface inherits operations from an employee interface.

To determine whether any objects in the personnel application can inherit characteristics, we must determine whether any objects are specific variants of other objects. So far, the application has four objects: employee, manager, personnel, and department. We begin by asking whether a department is an employee or a manager. The answer, of course, is No. But when we ask whether a manager is an employee or a department, the answer is Yes and No. A manager is a kind of an employee, but a manager is not a kind of department. Therefore, the manager object could inherit behavior from an employee object.

For information on how to define inheritance in OMG IDL, see Chapter 7.

## 5.4.1  An Example Use of Interface Inheritance

In our personnel framework, we have examined what happens when an employee is transferred and found that the process requires the approval of a manager. To add this process to our real-world model of the transfer operation, we add a Manager object to the model that has an approve_transfer operation.

A manager is like any other employee, except that the manager has the additional ability to approve transfers. Therefore, the Manager object can inherit behavior from the Employee object. Figure 5–1 illustrates how the Manager object inherits the promote, dismiss, and transfer operations from the Employee object.

**Figure 5–1  A Conceptual Look at Interface Inheritance**

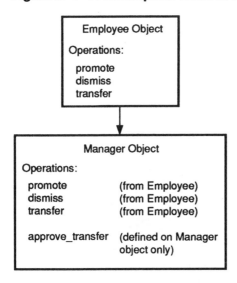

ZK-7728A

### 5.4.2  Using Multiple Inheritance

Objects can inherit behavior from more than one object; this process is called **multiple inheritance**. You should use multiple inheritance with restraint, because it adds complexity to your design and is something that is not often needed. Developers tend to use multiple inheritance only when they need to create some very specialized composite object types.

An object that inherits behavior from multiple objects is affected by any change to any object it inherits from. Therefore, you need to make sure the objects that you are inheriting from do not conflict in any way; such conflicts could cause unpredictable results in your model.

By expanding the example of single inheritance, we can examine how multiple inheritance works. The Employee object has the promote, dismiss, and transfer operations defined on it. Two kinds of objects represent specialized types of employees: a Manager object, which can approve transfers between departments, and a Personnel object, which can hire employees. So it makes sense for both objects to inherit from the Employee object.

Personnel representatives have special capabilities that other employees do not. Therefore, Corporate Services needs a special kind of manager for them, a personnel manager. A personnel manager has the capabilities of both a personnel employee and a manager. Thus, we decide to model the personnel manager as an object that inherits from both the Manager object and the Personnel object. And because a personnel manager in Corporate Services has the ability to arbitrate disputes between employees, the arbitrate operation is added as a unique operation to the PersonnelManager object.

Figure 5–2 shows how the PersonnelManager object inherits the approve_transfer operation from the Manager object and the hire operation from the Personnel object.

## 5.5  Using Operations and Attributes Effectively

In CORBA, **object attributes** as well as operations can manipulate objects. This section defines an object attribute and provides guidelines for when to use object attributes and operations.

Figure 5–2  A Conceptual Look at Multiple Inheritance

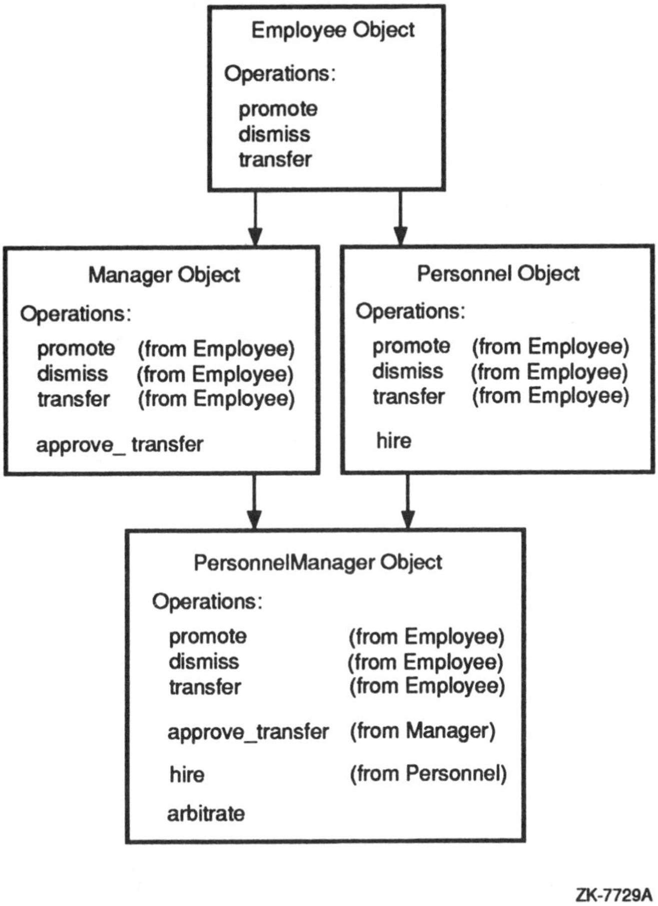

```
                    ┌────────────────────────┐
                    │    Employee Object      │
                    │                          │
                    │  Operations:             │
                    │                          │
                    │    promote               │
                    │    dismiss               │
                    │    transfer              │
                    └────────────────────────┘
                         │              │
                         ▼              ▼
┌─────────────────────────────┐  ┌─────────────────────────────┐
│      Manager Object          │  │      Personnel Object        │
│                               │  │                               │
│  Operations:                  │  │  Operations:                  │
│                               │  │                               │
│   promote   (from Employee)   │  │   promote   (from Employee)   │
│   dismiss   (from Employee)   │  │   dismiss   (from Employee)   │
│   transfer  (from Employee)   │  │   transfer  (from Employee)   │
│                               │  │                               │
│   approve_ transfer           │  │   hire                        │
└─────────────────────────────┘  └─────────────────────────────┘
                         │              │
                         ▼              ▼
              ┌──────────────────────────────────────┐
              │      PersonnelManager Object           │
              │                                         │
              │  Operations:                            │
              │                                         │
              │    promote          (from Employee)     │
              │    dismiss          (from Employee)     │
              │    transfer         (from Employee)     │
              │                                         │
              │    approve_transfer (from Manager)      │
              │                                         │
              │    hire             (from Personnel)    │
              │                                         │
              │    arbitrate                            │
              └──────────────────────────────────────┘
```

ZK-7729A

## 5.5.1  What Is an Object Attribute?

An object attribute is a very basic operation on the object. In fact, when you specify an object attribute in OMG IDL, the object attribute converts to a routine that is very similar to the routine an operation converts to when the operation is mapped to its C binding. Object attributes also return the standard exceptions that CORBA defines; however, they do not return user-defined exceptions.

You can use an object attribute to get and set data that is associated with an object. The value of the object attribute describes the data. For example, the value of the object attribute employee_badge would be the employee's badge number, such as 1239.

You can define one or two routines for an object attribute: one routine to retrieve (get) the value of the object attribute and another to enter (set) the value of the object attribute. By default, values can be retrieved or entered into all object attributes, unless you declare the attribute as read-only, in which case only the routine that retrieves the attribute's value is available. Both routines map to methods within the associated implementation.

For information on how to define object attributes in OMG IDL, see Chapter 7.

## 5.5.2 When to Use Object Attributes or Operations

If you need to retrieve and enter a single piece of data in your application, it does not matter whether you use object attributes or operations to do it. However, if your application is working with multiple pieces of data, there are situations when it is best to use an object attribute and others when it is best to use an operation.

It is appropriate to use an object attribute when your application:

- Requires read-only access to data

  For example, an employee locator facility that displays data on the office location and phone number of employees would work well as an object attribute.

- Requires simple entry or retrieval of data rather than a complex task

  For example, the process "get employee personal data" lends itself nicely to an object attribute. However, the process "get sales summary for 1994" does not work well as an object attribute because it is far more complex. Getting the sales summary for 1994 requires additional information from multiple sources rolled into some form of summary report. Such information might be: the kinds of sales results, whether it is for the calendar year or fiscal year, and when the fiscal year begins and ends.

It is better to use operations when the process of entering or retrieving data for your application has the following restrictions:

- Requires additional input, such as formal arguments or propagated context

- Is more complex than retrieving or entering a data item within some kind of data storage

- Requires the return of a failure condition that is not covered by the standard exceptions

## 5.5.3 When to Use Read-Only Object Attributes

When you want to allow client applications to retrieve, but not enter, information using the object attribute, you mark an object attribute as readonly. One situation in which you might want to do this is when the process of entering the data is more complex than simply assigning a new value to the attribute.

For example, you might define a department object attribute as read-only to reflect the fact that end users can retrieve, but not change, an employee's department. Changing an employee's department might be modeled as transferring an employee and might involve an extended process that includes removing the employee from his or her current department, assigning the employee to another department, and getting approval for the transfer from the managers of both departments.

In this case, it is easy to represent finding an employee's department name or number, but it is not easy to represent changing an employee's department. Therefore, it is more efficient to represent the retrieval of the information as a read-only object attribute and the entry of the information as another operation (transfer operation).

# 6

# Considerations in Distributing Your Design

Now that you have created a model of your application or framework and decided which pieces of your application or framework to distribute, you need to take into account the following factors that might affect your design:

- How to refine your model for a distributed environment

- How to select an **interaction model** that most efficiently allows the components to work the way you intend them to work

- How to determine the packaging of your application

This chapter describes these factors as they apply to designing a CORBA application or framework. In this chapter, distributing an application or framework refers to dividing the software into separate pieces that run as separate processes or threads on different machines across a network. This chapter does not discuss how to distribute the pieces of your application onto one or more computer systems; this is a deployment issue that we discuss in Chapter 11.

## 6.1 Refining Your Model for a Distributed Environment

When designing an application or framework, it is important to refine your model to ensure that the application or framework works easily and effectively in a distributed environment. If you are building an application or framework on top of CORBA, you are typically building a distributed object-oriented system of some kind. When you design such a system, you need to make distribution part of the design. If you do not, you can produce a model that is architecturally sound, but that performs poorly because a lot of network calls are used.

This section lists some of the common refinements of a distributed object-oriented system.

### 6.1.1 Accounting for Remote Operations

In a nondistributed system, all objects and operations are in a single process. You can call many objects and operations numerous times with little or no impact on performance. However, when objects are distributed across the network, you need to minimize the number of requests that you make to remote objects to ensure optimum performance.

For example, suppose you are modeling a text editor to be built on the CORBA system. The model for the text editor divides it into two logical parts: the client is the user interface that presents the text editor to the end user, and the server is the engine that does the actual work. Each end-user keystroke is a separate request from the text editor client that causes the implementation on the server to perform some function, such as moving the cursor or opening a menu. While this model works fine in a nondistributed environment, it becomes cumbersome in a distributed environment. Performance is seriously affected if you place the server on a powerful computer at a remote location on the network and the client on local user machines. The system sends each keystroke across the network and end users must wait to type after every couple of keystrokes.

### 6.1.2 Adding Levels of Interface Abstraction

Clients and servers in a CORBA-based system communicate by sending client requests for operations on objects to servers that perform those requests. You describe these operations and their associated objects in various interfaces, which you can model at many different levels of abstraction.

Abstraction is the process of thinking about a group of items in a more general way. In software, we use abstraction to make generalizations that let us focus on what we want to do, rather than on how it is actually done. For example, with the distributed text editor, the design called for the text editor to send requests for operations on keystroke objects from the client to the server. Using something more abstract and useful, such as menus, functions, or even buffers, would increase performance and eliminate unnecessary detail.

### 6.1.3 Separating User Interactions from Data Interactions

A more common need for distribution arises when your application has one or more user interfaces. You can distribute user interface components in any way you choose, depending upon the needs of the application. For example, you can split your user interface into multiple clients or servers, each handling a certain portion of the user interface, such as displaying online information or creating and dismissing dialog boxes. The most common distribution technique, however, is based on the separation of user interactions from data interactions. An application's user interactions are the visual presentation of the application to an end user. An application's data interactions are the tasks the application does.

For example, suppose you must extend the text editor for the personnel application to handle three natural languages: English, German, and Kanji. To extend the editor, you could decide to have a separate text editing interface for each natural language and one text processing engine. Figure 6–1 shows this division of user and data interactions.

**Figure 6–1  The Text Editor Distributed by User and Data Interactions**

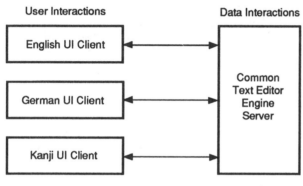

ZK-7730A

Distributing an application by user and data interactions can optimize performance. The user interfaces perform well because they are local to their end users and are freed from the overhead of doing the work of the application's engine. The engine performs well because it does not handle the end-user interface and because it is typically on a system that has the capacity to handle such compute-intensive applications.

You could also divide the end user and data interactions by using one user interface that uses multiple engines. For example, suppose a distributed debugger has a single user interface running on a laptop. This interface lets users debug applications on many different operating systems and in many different programming languages. The debugger is also distributed by separating its user interactions on the laptop from its data interactions on the various server platforms, as shown in Figure 6–2.

**Figure 6–2 The Debugger Distributed by User and Data Interactions**

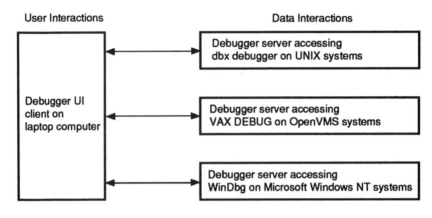

ZK-7731A

In this distributed debugger, the user interface client on the laptop is purely a display mechanism; it contains few or no debugger functions. Instead, the client sends requests across the network to the particular servers it needs to contact. To have something to display, the debugger user interface depends on information that the debugger servers send and receive.

## 6.1.4 Adding Convenience Functions

Adding an operation or an object to optimize your model is fine as long as you do not compromise the abilities or the interface abstraction of your application. When you have begun to build the model, you may find it is cumbersome to program in certain circumstances. If so, you may need to add some kind of convenience functions to your application and your model. For example, suppose you would like to use the database from the corporate personnel example to build a distributed employee locator system that allows any employee to look up the location of any other employee at any of several buildings. To access this system, employees need to supply their name, badge number, and date of hire (for simple authentication).

The model for this application requires that the system send a separate request to obtain each of the three pieces of employee information. Because an employee can look up data from any site, your employee database is not likely to be on an employee's local system. Thus, each request for information will require a roundtrip network call between the client and the server application. To avoid making three calls each time an employee accesses the system, you could add a convenience function: an additional operation on the employee object, such as employee_get_ident, that requests the three pieces of data in a single call. This new operation actually makes the application faster and easier to code, and has no meaningful effect on the architectural model for the application.

## 6.2 Selecting an Interaction Model

An interaction model describes how the clients and servers in your distributed application or application framework work with each other. Selecting an interaction model is part of designing a distributed application, whether you are designing a single distributed application, several distributed applications, or a distributed framework that makes use of several applications.

Distributed applications are applications that are distributed across two or more computers that are connected by a network. Although CORBA tends to be used for applications and application frameworks that work across multiple systems on a network, not all CORBA applications need to be distributed across the network. A CORBA application could have the client and server as separate processes on the same system. Another application might have a CORBA server that is actually a dynamically linked library into which the CORBA client has linked their address space at run time.

In this section, we will look at some of the more popular interaction models and explain why an application or framework would use each of them. These models include the following:

- Classic interaction model
- Peer-to-peer interaction model
- Broker interaction model

### 6.2.1 Classic Interaction Model

The classic interaction model is the most common view of client/server computing. In the classic interaction model, the client and server have a requester and responder relationship. The client is always the requester, requesting the server to perform a task, and the server is always the responder that performs the requested task. Typically, in the classic interaction model, the client is the controlling part of the application, and the server is little more than a set of remote functions. Distributed applications that use RPC commonly use this model. Because the client in this model is the controlling portion of the application, the client tends to be more complex and composed of many more lines of code than the server, which simply responds in a predetermined way to the requests the client sends to it.

**When to Use the Classic Interaction Model** A good time to use the classic model is when there is a clear separation of the controlling and the controlled portions of the application. An example of this would be an application that is separated by form and function; that is, an application that is divided into a client portion that handles the presentation of the application to the end user (the form) and a server portion that handles the actual processing of the data (the function). In this case, the client is responsible not only for managing the **graphical user interface** but also for transforming the end user's responses to the user interface into requests that the client can send to a server.

**Example Use of the Classic Interaction Model** Let's now model our example personnel application using the classic interaction model. End users in the personnel department use this distributed application. The client portion of the application handles all dealings with the personnel end user, including handling the display of the user interface to the end user, generating reports for the end user, and gathering information from the end user. Once the client has enough information to form a request, the client constructs and sends that request to a server. The server then performs the requested task (perhaps by looking up employee information in some remote database), and sends the result of the task back to the client, which displays the resulting data to the end user.

## 6.2.2 Peer-to-Peer Interaction Model

In the peer-to-peer interaction model, the client and the server are cooperating applications that can request services from, and provide services to, each other. In the peer-to-peer interaction model, there is no real distinction between clients and servers—in this model, all applications act both as clients that request services and servers that provide those services. Such peer applications can be independent applications, possibly with individual user interfaces. In CORBA, each peer contains both client and server portions of code. The client portions invoke requests for operations and the server portions respond to the requests for operations.

There are two key differences between the classic and peer-to-peer interaction models:

- Relationship between the client and the server

   In the classic interaction model, applications have unequal abilities and a requester/responder relationship; whereas, in a peer-to-peer interaction model, applications have equal abilities and work together equally.

- Complexity

  Peer-to-peer applications are more complex than a dedicated server or a dedicated client that uses the classic interaction model to perform similar functions because the peer-to-peer model requires each application to be both a client and a server.

Which model is best depends on your particular framework needs.

**When to Use the Peer-To-Peer Interaction Model** The peer-to-peer model is appropriate to use when you need your client and server to cooperate to achieve the desired results. For example, suppose that you cannot place all control for the distributed application in the client because, under certain circumstances, the server needs to make the client perform some tasks. In such a case, you need to adopt the peer-to-peer model because the classic interaction model does not allow the server to act as a client.

On the other hand, if your applications act as only clients or servers, but never as both, then you can use either a classic or peer-to-peer interaction model, depending on which best suits your needs.

**Example Use of the Peer-To-Peer Interaction Model** Let's now model our personnel framework using the peer-to-peer interaction model. In this example, we want to illustrate the idea of peer applications, so we will extend our example personnel framework to include three cooperating applications. Each application was originally a department-specific distributed application that used the classic interaction model, but the company has upgraded these systems so that they can interact in a peer-to-peer fashion.

The three cooperating applications are:

- Personnel Employee Application (PEA)

  Personnel employees use the PEA to enter and modify employee information such as job codes, cost centers, and so on, and to generate reports based on this information.

- Security Employee Application (SEA)

  Security employees use the SEA to enter and modify security information such as employee clearances, restricted areas, and so on, and to generate reports based on this information.

- Authorization Approval Application (AAA)

  Managers of both the security and personnel departments use the AAA to enter and modify security information such as which employees can access certain types of information that deal with high-level security clearances, sensitive employee data, and so on, and to generate reports based on this information.

The PEA, SEA, and AAA not only request that servers provide, update, or delete information, but they can also respond to requests for information from each other.

### 6.2.3 Broker Interaction Model

In the broker interaction model, a specialized server called a broker acts as an intermediary between one or more clients and one or more servers in your distributed system. A broker represents a client when the client makes a request to a server and represents a server when a server makes a response to a client.

Be careful not to confuse the broker interaction model with CORBA or the ORB. They are not the same things, even though both acronyms expand into phrases that contain the word broker. You could just as easily call the broker interaction model the intermediary server interaction model or something else. The important distinction is that a broker is a *specialized server* that acts as a go-between between one or more clients and one or more servers. In contrast, the ORB is a CORBA *component* that handles the distribution of requests to implementations that can handle them.

Brokering is a general problem-solving technique used in distributed computing. Brokering is not used solely with CORBA or with object-oriented systems.

**When to Use the Broker Interaction Model** You tend to use brokering when you have environments in which you have many servers that need to be coordinated for some reason, or when you want greater logical separation between your clients and servers.

You can insert a broker into either the classic or peer-to-peer interaction models, as long as your distributed system allows it (CORBA does). Some distributed systems have clients hardwired into servers so that you cannot insert a broker between the two, but this is not the case with CORBA.

When you use a broker interaction model in a non-CORBA system, the client sends one or more requests to the broker and the broker then sends the request to the server based on some criteria. For example, a broker might be a print server that can handle printing requests (the criteria might be that the printer is a laser printer, a plotter, a color printer, or a specific printer location, and so on).

When you use a broker interaction model in a CORBA system, there are two intermediaries: the ORB and the broker. The ORB serves as an intermediary for requests; the broker handles access to services. When a client sends a request, it might be directed through the ORB to a broker, which then sends the request to the appropriate server. Although the ORB is based on brokering techniques, the ORB does not have all the capabilites of a broker. For example, an ORB, unlike a broker, cannot handle load balancing (such as selecting the least busiest printer), and some ORBs cannot handle criteria-based selection (such as a request for a color laser printer at a particular location). The use of a broker in a CORBA system simplifies the writing of the client code because the broker contains the criteria for server selection.

Figure 6–3 illustrates the use of a broker in a CORBA system and a non-CORBA system.

**Figure 6–3  A Broker In a CORBA and Non-CORBA System**

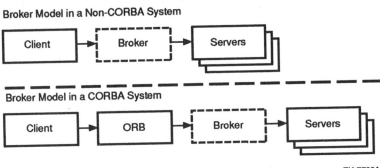

ZK-7732A

Note that in either the general or the CORBA-specific case, the broker needs to know how to access the servers that it supports. This information about the servers could be the actual location of the servers on the network, or, in an object-oriented system like CORBA, it could be a reference to that server object.

There are two common brokering schemes that tend to be used with brokers:

- Introduction brokering, whereby the broker locates a server for a client and lets the client and server communicate

- Routing brokering, whereby the broker locates a server for a client and handles all communication between the client and server

You can use either or both schemes in your distributed environment, depending on your needs. The following sections describe these two schemes.

### 6.2.3.1 Introduction Brokering

In an introduction brokering scheme, active servers register with the broker to make themselves known in the system. The client can then send a message to the broker asking for a server that can perform some task. The introduction broker selects a server to perform the task and returns information to the client for accessing that server. That is, the broker introduces the server to the client, but the client and the server contact each other directly. You can think of the broker in an introduction brokering scheme as being a "phonebook" server; the client accesses the phonebook server to get the phone number of the server it wants to call.

**When to Use Introduction Brokering**   You can generally use introduction brokering when clients or servers in your system need to be introduced to other servers in the system. This situation occurs when you do not want, or cannot have, all your clients and servers know about each other, such as when you have a system in which the clients and servers are constantly starting and stopping for various reasons.

Introduction brokering is also useful for load balancing in a distributed system. For example, if you have three servers that can process a client's request, the broker can select the server that has the most available resources to handle that request.

**Example Use of the Introduction Brokering Model**   Let's now model our personnel framework using a broker and an introduction brokering scheme. When we discussed the peer-to-peer interaction model, we discussed three cooperating applications that the security and personnel departments use (the PEA, SEA, and AAA). When the PEA client needs security or authorization information, it contacts the SEA and AAA applications to get that information.

Because one of the reasons to use brokers is to coordinate multiple related servers in a distributed system, let's extend our example so that there are multiple security servers and security databases in our system, one for each facility that our company operates. Now we have a reason to add a broker to our example.

The following describes how to use the introduction broker in both a non-CORBA example and a CORBA example:

- In a non-CORBA example, when the PEA needs security information related to some employee, it needs to go to any of several servers to get that information. Without an introduction brokering scheme, the PEA client would need to contain the code needed to access all of these separate databases, which would increase its complexity. By using an introduction brokering scheme, the PEA client can send its request for security information to one place, the broker. The broker then analyzes the request and returns to the PEA client the information it needs to access the particular server that contains the information it requires. The PEA client could then directly access that server.

- Using the same example with a CORBA system, if the PEA client made a request for security information on some employee, the ORB would pass the request to the broker that has the security information needed for the request. The broker would select the appropriate server, return to the ORB the information needed to access the server, and the ORB would directly access that server.

In both cases, we have isolated the knowledge of where the security servers are located to the broker. Neither the client nor the ORB needs to contain this information.

### 6.2.3.2  Routing Brokering

In a routing brokering scheme, the client sends a message to the broker asking for a server that can perform some task. The routing broker then selects a server to perform the task and sends the client's request to that server. The broker handles all communication; no direct communication between the client and the server ever takes place.

The primary difference between the introduction and routing brokering schemes is how communication takes place. With an introduction broker, the broker introduces the client and server, which then communicate directly with one another. With a routing broker, the client and server communicate only with the broker and never directly with each other.

This separation between the client and the server makes the routing brokering scheme powerful. Because of this separation, a client or server needs to have knowledge only of the broker; the clients and servers do not need any information about other clients and servers in the system.

**When to Use Routing Brokering**  Routing brokering is useful in large systems with many clients and servers. The centralization of information about the servers makes it much easier to update information about them. The centralization also lets the broker potentially perform other tasks, such as load balancing between clients and servers to optimize performance, just as it does with the introduction brokering scheme.

Routing brokering also enables a single client or server to deal with multiple clients or servers simultaneously, without those clients or servers being aware that they are dealing with multiple entities. The clients or servers only know that they are dealing with the broker.

**Example Use of the Routing Brokering Model**  Let's now describe an example using the routing brokering scheme just as we did for the introduction brokering scheme, using our three applications, the PEA, SEA, and AAA. Again, let's assume that there are multiple security servers and security databases in our system. However, because these databases contain sensitive information, we have designed our system so that there is a formal separation between the clients and servers. Our system uses a routing brokering scheme to achieve this separation.

Using a routing brokering scheme makes the server more secure because the client never directly contacts the server and also simplifies the coding of the clients. The clients do not need to know how to access any other servers except for the routing broker, and they also do not need to contain code to determine which server they need to access. The routing broker takes care of it all. In addition, the routing broker could provide other features for the distributed system, such as load balancing, error recovery, and so on.

As with the introduction brokering scheme, the routing broker would exist between the client and the server in a non-CORBA environment and between the ORB and the server in a CORBA environment. In either case, the routing broker formally separates the client from the server, so they never directly contact each other.

# 6.3 Popular Applications of Interaction Models

The following are some popular forms of the interaction models that we've already discussed. They are described here to give you ideas for other possible uses for these interaction models:

- Desktop launch (classic interaction model)

  The desktop launch model uses the classic interaction model where only the client can request a server to perform a task. This model is useful to use when the framework must allow an end user to start some application remotely from some desktop environment. Although useful, the desktop launch interaction model is a fairly restricted model. However, it does have the advantage of being simple.

  In the desktop launch model, the client has a graphical user interface desktop of some kind. The end user clicks on an icon on this desktop to launch or start an application. When the end user clicks on the icon, the client sends a request to a server to start the application.

The desktop launch interaction model is restrictive because it only allows for one-way communication between the client and the server, and because it will send only a start request. There is no further interaction between the client and server. The client just assumes that the application was successfully started and expects no success or failure to be returned from the server.

- Database server (routing brokering model)

  The database server model uses a broker interaction model with a routing brokering scheme specialized for use with databases. This model is useful to use when the framework must insulate the client from the various types of databases and database access mechanisms being used. In effect, this model hides the source of the data.

  In the database server model, the client requests some data from the database server (the routing broker). The database server then sends the request in the correct form to the database that contains the required information. Depending on the information the client requests, the database server might need to send an SQL select expression to a relational database or access a remote directory of files to get the requested information.

  Upon receipt of the information from the database, the database server then returns the information to the client, without the client ever knowing how the information was retrieved or stored.

- Object factory (classic, peer-to-peer, or broker interaction models)

  The object factory model features a special-purpose server. You can use this model with the classic, peer-to-peer, or broker interaction models. The object factory model is useful to use for object-oriented frameworks where you want a server that does nothing but create and return new objects for your system.

  In this model, a client application sends a request to a server for it to perform an operation on some object. The server, knowing that this object does not yet exist, sends a request to the object factory server asking it to create this object and return a reference to the new object. The object factory creates the object and returns a reference to it to the server, which performs the operation and sends the result to the client.

## 6.4 Using the Interaction Models with Your Framework

One, or a combination of several, of these interaction models should fit the needs of your framework. For example, you could use the peer-to-peer interaction model with several specialized servers, such as a database server. Or, you could use the classic interaction model with a broker inserted into it. You could even use multiple brokers in your model if it is complex enough.

If none of these model combinations fits your framework, then you can at least use these models as ideas for designing your own interaction model. These are just suggestions and are not the only models that you can use or that are best for your framework. However, when you discard each of these models, it is probably useful to note why they do not work for your framework so you can gain a better understanding of the interaction model you need and why you need it.

## 6.5 Determining How to Package Applications

In CORBA, an application can be only a client, only a server, or both a client and server. Accordingly, you can package your distributed application as a client-only kit, a server-only kit, a combined client and server kit, or all three, with each kit available on various platforms.

If possible, you need to consider how to package your kits when designing and developing your application. Thinking about how you can subdivide and sell your product early in the design process will make building the installation kits for your finished product significantly easier.

For example, if you decide during the design phase to sell a client-only package, you can design and build the client portion of your distributed application as a module that is easily separated from the rest of the system. If you make this decision after the distributed application is completed, you might need to change the application to separate the client from the rest of the system, which could prove very difficult to do.

# 7

# Coding with OMG IDL

This chapter contains information on coding your object model in OMG IDL, including guidelines for the following:

- Writing basic OMG IDL code
- Defining object attributes
- Defining inheritance
- Defining exceptions
- Defining context objects

Throughout this chapter and book, there are numerous examples of OMG IDL code so that can you become familiar with it; however, this is not a complete reference to OMG IDL. See the vendor of your CORBA system for detailed OMG IDL reference information.

For a complete listing of the OMG IDL code example used in this chapter as well as C and C++ code examples, see Appendix A.

## 7.1 General Guidelines for Writing OMG IDL Code

OMG IDL code is similar to C++ code, so if you are experienced in reading C or C++ code, you will see many similarities to the OMG IDL code in this chapter.

Example 7–1 shows a partial OMG IDL source file for the personnel application designed in Chapter 4. This source file shows how to code some of the basic elements of an object model, including objects, operations on the objects, and arguments to the operations. The numbered text that follows this example and other examples in the book provides an explanation of the items correspondingly numbered in the example code.

**Example 7-1  An OMG IDL Source File Fragment From the Personnel Application**

```
/* Personnel Application OMG IDL Source File
   File:  CORP.IDL  */
module CORP ❶
{
// Declarations of variables used throughout this module
   typedef long BadgeNum; ❷
   typedef long DeptNum;
   enum DismissalCode { DISMISS_FIRED, DISMISS_QUIT };
   .
   .
   .
// Interface Definitions
   interface Employee ❸
      {
      void promote ❶ ( in      char          new_job_class);
      void dismiss  ( in      DismissalCode  reason, ❺
                      in      string         description);
      }; // end of interface Employee
   .
   .
   .
}; /* end module CORP */
```

❶ Module name

   The module CORP contains the interfaces that are used throughout the corporation in this module. It is a good programming practice to put OMG IDL code for related interfaces in modules, although the OMG IDL syntax does not require it. This avoids name clashes between other service groups or organizations within your corporation or enterprise. You should not confuse modules with files, which contain OMG IDL code.

❷ Declarations

   BadgeNum, DeptNum, and DismissalCode are some of the declarations that apply to the interfaces and operations in this module.

❸ Start of the interface definition for the Employee interface

   In OMG IDL, the keyword interface is used to define a kind of object. An object description includes any attributes and operations that can be performed on an object. An object description is called an interface definition in OMG IDL.

❶ Operation name

The lines beginning with void promote and void dismiss define the two operations available on the Employee interface. The operation name is preceded with the data type for the data being returned. In this example, the void data type means that the operation does not have any function return value.

❺ Definition for the dismiss operation

This definition creates the signature associated with the dismiss operation. The signature for an operation includes the following:

— The order of the arguments.

— The **direction attribute,** which indicates whether the client or the server can modify the associated argument. The direction attribute is similar to a passing mode in most programming languages. The direction attribute is listed first in an argument definition. Valid direction attributes are in, out, or inout.

— The data types of the argument. The data type of an argument, such as char or string, is listed second in an argument definition.

— Argument name.

— Return value, if any, which includes a result and possible outcome, such as normal, which indicates success, and exceptional, which indicates an error.

In the code example, the dismiss operation on the Employee interface has the following signature:

— Two arguments: reason and description.

— A direction attribute for each argument: the example specifies the direction attribute in for both the reason and description arguments, indicating that the method in the server cannot modify the arguments. If the method in the server returns data to the client, you need to specify the direction attribute out. If the method on the server cannot alter the data type, but it can update the value at run time, you need to specify the direction attribute inout. For more information on direction attributes, see Table 8–2 in Chapter 8.

- — A data type for each argument: DismissalCode is the data type for the reason argument and string is the data type for the description argument.

- — No return value: the dismiss operation is specified as a void and, therefore, does not return a value.

# 7.2 Defining Object Attributes in OMG IDL

When using object attributes to get and set data associated with an object, you need to decide how to model the object data. You can model the object data in one of two ways:

- Simple data types with single attributes, such as a string, char, or float for the object attribute

  This method is useful if you want to get or set the information represented by the object attribute one piece at a time.

- Complex data types containing one or more groups of data, such as a structure for the object attribute

  This method is useful if you want to use a single call to get or set the information represented by the object attribute in a group.

What is best for each application can vary considerably. If the pieces of data are not related to each other in any useful way, it is easier to use a simple data type. On the other hand, if the pieces are related and you usually expect your application to retrieve the information from a remote location, then you might want to group your data into a complex data type so the application can retrieve all the information over the network in a single call.

For more information on object attributes, see Chapter 5.

## 7.2.1 Specifying Object Attributes

Example 7–2 is a continuation of the previous OMG IDL code fragment that now shows the DeptID object attribute, which has a data type of DeptInfo.

**Example 7–2  Defining an Object Attribute in OMG IDL**

```
/* Personnel Application OMG IDL Source File
   File:  CORP.IDL  */

module CORP
{
// Declarations of variables used throughout this module
    typedef long        BadgeNum;
    typedef long        DeptNum;
    enum DismissalCode { DISMISS_FIRED, DISMISS_QUIT };
    .
    .
    .

// Declarations of data for data types
    .
    .
    .
    struct DeptInfo ❶
        {
        DeptNum     id;
        string      name;
        };
// Interface Definitions
    interface Department
        {
        attribute DeptInfo    DeptID; ❷
        }; // end of interface Department
}; // end module CORP
```

❶ Definition of a data structure used to represent department information

The struct DeptInfo section defines the structure used to represent department information: the department ID and name. This structure is a complex data type structure composed of two individual, but related, simple data types (department ID and name).

❷ Object attribute definition

The Department interface defines one object attribute: DeptID with a data type of DeptInfo. This attribute defines the ability to both retrieve and set department information using the data structure DeptInfo.

## 7.2.2 Specifying Read-Only Object Attributes

Example 7–3 continues the previous code example fragment and now shows two object attributes for the Department interface.

**Example 7–3 Specifying a Read-Only Object Attribute in OMG IDL**

```
/* Personnel Application OMG IDL Source File
   File:  CORP.IDL  */

module CORP
{
// Forward declaration for interfaces
interface Employee;
    .
    .
    .
// Declarations of data for data types
    struct DeptInfo
        {
        DeptNum         id;
        string          name;
        };
// Interface Definitions
    interface Department
        {
                attribute DeptInfo    DeptID;  ❶
        readonly attribute Employee   manager_obj;  ❷
        }; // end of interface Department
    interface Employee
        {
                attribute EmpData      personal_data;
        readonly attribute Department  department_obj;
            .
            .
            .
        }; // end of interface Employee
    .
    .
    .
}; // end module CORP
```

❶ Read and write object attribute

This line specifies the DeptID object attribute as modifiable, which means that client applications can use this attribute type to retrieve and enter information. The struct DeptInfo line defines the structure of each piece of data for the DeptID object attribute.

❷ Read-only object attribute

This line specifies the manager_obj object attribute as a read-only data type through the use of the readonly identifier. This specification allows client applications to retrieve, but not enter, information using this attribute type.

# 7.3 Defining Inheritance in OMG IDL

There are two forms of inheritance:

- Single inheritance—An interface inherits characteristics from another interface

- Multiple inheritance—An interface inherits characteristics from two or more interfaces

When coding for inheritance, you must define the interface to be inherited from before you define the interface that is to inherit from it. That is, if you are defining the interfaces in an OMG IDL file, you must precede the inheriting interface with the interface to be inherited from or declare the interface to be inherited from in a forward declaration. The same is true for defining data types in an OMG IDL file. If you are storing the interface definitions in an interface repository, then the interface that is being inherited from must already exist in the interface repository.

The following examples show how to write OMG IDL code for each type of inheritance. For more information on object inheritance, see Chapter 5.

## 7.3.1 Specifying Single Inheritance

Example 7–4, a continuation of the OMG IDL code for the personnel application, shows single inheritance for interfaces. In this example, the personnel interface definition stores employee information in two areas: PersonalData, which contains nonconfidential data for general use, and EmpData, which contains confidential data that has restricted access. This example also includes a manager interface.

### Example 7–4  Specifying Single Inheritance

```
/* Personnel Application OMG IDL Source File
   File:  CORP.IDL  */

module CORP
{
    .
    .
    .

// Declarations of data for data types
    struct PersonalData  ❶
        {
        string              last_name;
        string              first_name;
        string              middle_name;
        string              phone;
        string              site;
        };
    typedef PersonalData    EmpPersonalData;  ❷
    struct EmpData
        {
        BadgeNum            id;
        EmpPersonalData     personal_info;
        char                job_class;
        float               hourly_rate;
        };
    .
    .
    .


// Interface Definitions
    interface Employee
        {
                 attribute EmpData        personal_data;  ❸
        readonly attribute Department     department_obj;
        void promote ( in   char          new_job_class);
        void dismiss ( in   DismissalCode  reason,
                       in   string         description);
        void transfer ( in  Department     new_dept_obj);
        }; // end of interface Employee
```

(continued on next page)

**Example 7-4 (Cont.)  Specifying Single Inheritance**

```
interface Manager : Employee ④
    {
    void approve_transfer ( in     Employee     employee_obj, ⑤
                            in     Department   current_department,
                            in     Department   new_department);
    }; // end of interface Manager
    .
    .
    .
}; // end module CORP
```

❶  Data type definition

The struct PersonalData section lists the pieces of data contained in the PersonalData data type: employee name, phone number, and site location. This is nonconfidential employee data that requires few access restrictions.

❷  Nested data type definition

The typedef PersonalData line defines the EmpPersonalData data type that is used as a member of the EmpData structure.

This line is followed by the struct EmpData section, which uses the EmpPersonalData data type. The employee ID, job class, and hourly rate are confidential employee pieces of data that require access restrictions.

❸  Object attribute definition

The Employee interface defines the personal_data object attribute, which returns information about an employee using the EmpData data type. You do not need to enter an attribute definition for the PersonalData data type because it is a nested data type member.

❹  Single interface inheritance

The syntax interface Manager : Employee indicates that the Manager interface inherits all the characteristics of the previously defined Employee interface. The inheritance includes all object attributes (personal_data and department_obj), operations (promote, dismiss, and transfer), typedefs, and so on, for the Employee interface.

❺  Additional operation for the inheriting interface

The Manager interface defines four operations: the promote, dismiss, and transfer operations it inherits from the Employee interface and the approve_transfer operation specified here for only the Manager interface.

## 7.3.2 Specifying Multiple Inheritance

Example 7–5 continues the OMG IDL code fragment showing multiple inheritance from both the Manager interface and the Personnel interface to the PersonnelManager interface.

**Example 7–5  Specifying Multiple Interface Inheritance**

```
/* Personnel Application OMG IDL Source File
   File:  CORP.IDL  */

module CORP
{
     .
     .
     .

    interface Employee
        {
                attribute EmpData           personal_data;
        readonly attribute Department       department_obj;
        void promote ( in  char             new_job_class);
        void dismiss ( in  DismissalCode     reason,
                       in  string           description);
        void transfer ( in  Department      new_dept_obj);
        }; // end of interface Employee

    interface Manager : Employee
        {
        void approve_transfer ( in  Employee     employee_obj,
                                in  Department    current_department,
                                in  Department    new_department);
        }; // end of interface Manager

    interface Personnel : Employee
        {
        Employee hire ( in   EmpData      employee_data,
                        in   Department   department_obj,
                        out  BadgeNum     new_employee_id);
        }; // end of interface Personnel
```

(continued on next page)

**Example 7–5 (Cont.)  Specifying Multiple Interface Inheritance**

```
interface PersonnelManager : Personnel, Manager ❶
    {
    void arbitrate ( ); ❷
        .
        .
        .
    }; // end of interface PersonnelManager
    .
    .
    .
}; // end module CORP
```

❶ Multiple interface inheritance

The syntax `interface PersonnelManager : Personnel, Manager` specifies that the `PersonnelManager` interface inherits behavior from both the `Personnel` and the `Manager` interfaces. These inherited operations include the `promote`, `dismiss`, `transfer`, and `approve_transfer` operations it inherits from the `Manager` interface and the `hire` operation it inherits from the `Personnel` interface.

❷ Additional operation for the inheriting interface

The code explicitly defines the `arbitrate` operation for the `PersonnelManager` interface.

## 7.3.3 Specifying Inheritance Across Modules

In addition to specifying inheritance within a module, you can also specify single and multiple inheritance across multiple modules for interfaces. For example, you might have a corporate personnel module for management of personnel in an entire corporation and a related personnel module for specific personnel issues in each department in the corporation, such as an engineering department. In this case, you might want the engineering manager interface to inherit all the characteristics of the corporate personnel manager interface and have specific additional characteristics as an engineering manager.

Example 7–6 continues the OMG IDL code fragment showing interface inheritance from the CORP module to the ENGINEERING module.

### Example 7–6  Specifying Inheritance Across Modules

```
/* Personnel Application OMG IDL Source File
   File:  CORP.IDL  */

module CORP
{
    .
    .
    .

// Declarations of data for data types
    struct PersonalData
        {
        string          last_name;
        string          first_name;
        string          middle_name;
        string          phone;
        string          site;
        };
    typedef PersonalData    EmpPersonalData;
    struct EmpData
        {
        BadgeNum         id;
        EmpPersonalData  personal_info;
        char             job_class;
        float            hourly_rate;
        };

// Interface Definitions
    interface Employee
        {
        .
        .
        .
        }; // end of interface Employee
    interface Manager : Employee
        {
        .
        .
        .
        }; // end of interface Manager
    interface Personnel : Employee
        {
        .
        .
        .
        }; // end of interface Personnel
```

(continued on next page)

**Example 7–6 (Cont.)  Specifying Inheritance Across Modules**

```
    interface PersonnelManager : Personnel, Manager
        {
        .
        .
        .
        }; // end of interface PersonnelManager
    .
    .
    .
}; // end module CORP
module ENGINEERING ❶
{
// Interface Definitions
    interface EmployeeLocator
        {
        void FindEngineer ( in   CORP::BadgeNum     id, ❷
                            out  CORP::PersonalData  info);
        };
    interface PersonnelManager : CORP::PersonnelManager ❸
        {
        };
}; // end module ENGINEERING
```

❶  Second module

This line shows the start of a second module ENGINEERING that contains
information specific to engineering.

❷  Data type referencing across modules

The FindEngineer operation inherits data from the CORP module,
specifically the BadgeNum and PersonalData data types.

These two lines show the use of the in and out direction attributes. The
line in CORP::BadgeNum id specifies that the method on the client can input
the badge number identifier for the employee from the CORP module. The
line out CORP::PersonalData info specifies that the employee locator will
output data from the PersonalData data structure in the CORP module.

❸  Multiple interface inheritance across modules

The line interface PersonnelManager : CORP::PersonnelManager specifies
that the PersonnelManager interface in the ENGINEERING module
inherits characteristics from the PersonnelManager interface in the CORP
module.

## 7.4 Defining Exceptions in OMG IDL

CORBA provides a mechanism, called raising an exception, for reporting errors to the client application when a problem occurs.

There are two kinds of exceptions that differ as follows:

- Standard exceptions
  - Defined by CORBA
  - Can be used during the processing of an operation
  - Either an implementation of an object or the ORB can raise
- User-defined exceptions
  - Defined by those who define operations and interfaces
  - Can be used during the processing of an operation
  - Only an implementation of an object can raise

In a C language binding, every request contains an environment argument as the third argument. You do not need to define the environment argument in OMG IDL because CORBA implicitly passes it with each request. The way you present the argument is dependent on the language being used. CORBA uses the environment argument to store information about exceptions, such as the kind of exception, the contents of the exception, and any additional information.

In C, the environment argument is a partially opaque structure for operations that contains at least one member that is named _major. The _major member indicates whether the request terminated successfully and, if not, whether the exception raised is a standard or user-defined exception. Other fields in the environment argument are useful for specifying which exception to signal and additional exception information.

Example 7–7 shows a segment of C code that illustrates the environment structure and the _major member.

### Example 7–7  Environment Structure in C

```
/* Environment Structure in C
     typedef struct CORBA_Environment
  {
         CORBA_exception_type _major;
  .
  .
  .
  } CORBA_Environment;
```

The application designer decides which exceptions to make available to which operations. Part III discusses the environment argument to a request. Chapter 8 explains how to handle exceptions in your client application and Chapter 9 explains how to raise an exception in your implementation methods.

## 7.4.1  Using Standard Exceptions

CORBA defines a set of standard exceptions that all CORBA vendors must support. Standard exceptions cover broad problems such as general internal ORB errors and memory problems. See Table C–1 for a description of these standard exceptions.

Either the ORB or the implementation of an object can raise standard exceptions for an operation. Because the CORBA system itself defines standard exceptions, they are automatically available for the ORB or the implementation to use. You do not need to do anything in your OMG IDL file to enable your operations or object attributes to use the standard exceptions. When you develop the code for the server side of your application, you specify the use of exceptions using the CORBA_BOA_set_exception routine as described in Chapter 9.

A standard exception contains the following information:

- Name of the exception being raised, such as NO_PERMISSION

- A minor code

  The minor code indicates the subcategory of the exception. CORBA specifies that you should provide this minor code, but leaves it up to each CORBA vendor to specify which values are associated with it and what those values mean. For example, you could associate the minor code NO_ACL_DEFINED with the NO_PERMISSION standard exception to indicate that an end user cannot use the attempted operation because the end user does not have the correct access control permissions defined.

- A completion status code

  The completion status codes provide additional information to the application that can be useful in determining whether to try the failed request again. There are three completion status codes:

  - CORBA_COMPLETED_YES, which indicates the object implementation completed processing before the exception was raised.

  - CORBA_COMPLETED_NO, which indicates the object implementation was never initiated before the exception was raised.

  - CORBA_COMPLETED_MAYBE, which indicates the status of the object implementation is not known.

With standard exceptions, the _major member of the environment argument will indicate CORBA_SYSTEM_EXCEPTION if the request does not terminate successfully and CORBA_NO_EXCEPTION if there was no exception raised.

### 7.4.2 Defining User-Defined Exceptions

User-defined exceptions allow you to raise exceptions that CORBA does not include with the standard exceptions. User-defined exceptions tend to be specific to a particular operation; for example, you could define HIRING_FREEZE and NO_SUCH_DEPT for the hire operation.

There are two key restrictions on defining user-defined exceptions:

- You can associate user-defined exceptions with operations, but not with object attributes.

- The implementation can raise user-defined exceptions, but not the ORB.

You define user-defined exceptions in OMG IDL using the following statement and clause:

- Use the exception statement to define a user-defined exception and to specify the information it can contain and return.

- Use the raises clause on an operation to identify one or more user-defined exceptions that an operation can return. User-defined exceptions can contain whatever information you find most useful; they do not need to return the same information as a standard exception.

With user-defined exceptions, the _major member of the environment argument will indicate CORBA_USER_EXCEPTION if the request does not terminate successfully.

Example 7–8 shows an OMG IDL code fragment that defines the exception
DENY_APPROVAL and associates it with the approve_transfer operation in the
Manager interface.

**Example 7–8  Defining User-Defined Exceptions**

```
/* Personnel Application OMG IDL Source File
   File:  CORP.IDL  */

module CORP
{
    .
    .
    .
    enum  DenyApprovalReasons     { REASON, CODES };  ❶
    exception DENY_APPROVAL  ❷
        {
        DenyApprovalReasons     reason;
        };
        .
        .
        .
    interface Manager : Employee
        {
        void approve_transfer ( in    Employee       employee_obj,
                                in    Department     current_department,
                                in    Department     new_department)
                                raises (DENY_APPROVAL);  ❸
        }; // end of interface Manager
    .
    .
    .
}; /* end module CORP */
```

❶ Valid reason codes

   This line lists the set of valid reason codes that the implementation of the
   object can return in the DENY_APPROVAL exception.

❷ exception statement

   The exception statement defines the user-defined exception DENY_APPROVAL.
   This exception has one member, DenyApprovalReasons reason, which
   contains a number that corresponds to a reason indicated in the valid
   reason codes for why the approval is denied.

③ raises clause

The raises clause associates the DENY_APPROVAL exception with the approve_transfer operation in the Manager interface. If you have more than one exception for a raises clause, you can enter them sequentially using commas to separate them.

# 7.5 Defining Context to Be Propagated in OMG IDL

The context clause is a mechanism for propagating information about preferences associated with a request, such as identifying the printers for an end user to the server that performs the operation on the object.

When you use the context clause to propagate context information:

- The information is valid only for the duration of the request invocation.

- The ORB or the client application can read from, or write to, the context object to describe the preferred environment for the request.

- The server application can read the context object to retrieve the preferences when performing the requested operation.

The context object contains a name-value pair called a property. When you use the context clause on an operation, the clause indicates to the ORB that it should look up the context property defined in the context clause and pass the property and its value to the implementation of the object each time a client requests the operation. You use the context interface to enable client application control of context properties and their values. CORBA does not specify whether the context object is returned by the server to the client. Chapter 8 describes the context interface.

Example 7–9 shows an OMG IDL code fragment that defines the context property (division), which is to be propagated when the approve_transfer operation in the Manager interface is requested. An error does not occur if the preperty is not found in the context object. In this case, the property name is not propagated to the server.

## Example 7-9  Specifying Context Objects

```
/* Personnel Application OMG IDL Source File
   File:  CORP.IDL  */

module CORP
{
    .
    .
    .
    interface Employee
        {
                attribute EmpData          personal_data;
        readonly attribute Department      department_obj;
        void promote ( in  char            new_job_class);
        void dismiss ( in  DismissalCode   reason,
                       in  string          description);
        void transfer ( in  Department     new_dept_obj);
        }; // end of interface Employee
    interface Manager : Employee
        {
        void approve_transfer ( in  Employee     employee_obj,
                                in  Department    current_department,
                                in  Department    new_department)
                                raises (DENY_APPROVAL)
                                context ("division"); ❶
        }; // end of interface Manager
    .
    .
    .
}; // end module CORP
```

❶ Context specification

The context line specifies "division" as the name of a property contained in the context object. The "division" property refers to the division of the company in which the manager works. When a client application invokes the approve_transfer operation on the Manager interface, the ORB propagates the context property and its value to the server where the server can read division information on the manager's division and take it into account when performing the operation. The context statement must follow the raises statement, if any exceptions are defined for an operation.

## 7.6  For More Information

For information on how to generate object or executable code from OMG IDL code, see Chapters 8 and 9.

# Part III

## For the Application Developer: Developing a CORBA Application Framework

Part III shows the application developer how to build an application or application framework to run in a CORBA environment.

- Chapter 8 describes how to develop a client within your application framework, and includes information on how to create a request and select which invocation style and type to use in your application framework.

- Chapter 9 describes how to develop a server within your application framework.

- Chapter 10 describes how to connect client operations to methods on the server.

In these chapters we'll discuss how to use IDL and C code to build and connect clients and servers in a CORBA system. However, these chapters are not complete discussions of either the IDL or C language and should not be considered as substitutes for reference manuals for either language.

# 8

# Developing the Client Side of the Application

The result of the design process is one or more OMG IDL files that contain the definitions of the objects and operations for the application. To develop the application, you must first write the code that invokes and handles requests for the operations on the objects that you have defined. This code constitutes the CORBA-specific part of the application.

Before you can write this code, however, you need to decide how to invoke requests and what communication style to use for the invocations. One factor that will influence your decisions is the environment in which your application will run. For example, if your CORBA application will run in a CORBA framework, some of these decisions might be made for you by the design of the framework.

This chapter describes these options and suggests when to use each option. These descriptions might lead you to conclude that you can use only one type of invocation and one style of communication in your application. In fact, you can and will probably need to use various combinations of the two in a CORBA application.

This chapter answers the following questions:

- What is the structure of a request?

- Which invocation communication style should I use?

- Which invocation communication type should I use?

- How do I build a simple client application?

- How do I build a more complex client application?

## 8.1 Structure of a Request

A CORBA client application can be thought of as simply a series of requests. All requests have three basic parts and two optional parts:

- The name of the requested operation

- A reference to a specific object on which the operation is to be performed (in C, this reference is the first argument, called the object reference)

  An object reference is a value that identifies a specific instance of an object in a CORBA application. You pass object references, rather than the objects themselves, between applications because passing objects themselves can be a very cumbersome process, and might not even be possible in some systems.

- A reference to the environment pseudo object, which stores and returns information about the success or failure of the request (in C, this reference is the second argument)

  The environment object is a special kind of object called a pseudo object that the CORBA system creates for use by the CORBA application developer.

- A reference to a context pseudo object (in C, this is the third argument)

  If the operation uses a context object, you need to get the object reference for the one you will use in this request. A context object represents information about the client, environment, or circumstances of a request that for some reason are not passed as parameters. For example, a context object might supply such information as the end user's preferences for printers, local symbols, or servers.

- Zero or more additional arguments specific to the operation being requested

### 8.1.1 C Language Mapping for a Request

Example 8–1 shows a C language mapping for a client stub request (brackets indicate optional information).

**Example 8–1   C Language Mapping for a Request**

```
/* C */
void operation-name
    (
    CORBA_Object          target-object,
    CORBA_Environment     * environment,
  [ CORBA_Context         context-object, ]
  [ other data type       other-argument, ...]

    );
```

Table 8–1 describes the arguments in Example 8–1.

**Table 8–1   Description of Arguments in a Request**

| Argument | Data Type | Description |
|---|---|---|
| target-object | Opaque input | Identifies the reference to the specific object on which the operation is to be performed. |
| * environment | Partially opaque output | Identifies the environment argument that can contain exception information to be used by the program. |
| context-object | Opaque input | Identifies the reference to the context object, if the operation was defined to use the context object. |
| other-argument | Varies by argument | Identifies zero or more additional arguments needed by this specific request. |

Each argument specific to an operation on an interface of a request has an associated direction attribute, which you specify in the interface definition of the requested operation (OMG IDL code). This attribute indicates how the argument will be passed between client and server and whether either the client or the server can modify the argument. Table 8–2 describes the three direction attributes.

**Table 8–2  Direction Attributes**

| Direction Attribute | Description |
|---|---|
| in | The client specifies the data type and value of the argument at run time. The server can look at the value, but cannot update it. In most cases in C, an argument with the in direction attribute will be passed by value. |
| out | The client specifies the data type at run time but not the value of the argument. The server provides the value at run time. In most cases in C, an argument with the out direction attribute will be passed by reference. |
| inout | The client specifies the data type and value of the argument at run time. The server cannot alter the data type, but it can update the value at run time. In most cases in C, an argument with the inout direction attribute will be passed by reference. |

# 8.2 Choosing an Invocation Communication Style

CORBA supports three communication styles for requests:

- Synchronous communication

- Deferred synchronous communication

- One-way communication

You select a communication style when you choose the invocation type that you want to use for a request. Recall that there are two invocation types: stub-style and dynamic invocation. Section 8.3 describes these invocation types in greater detail.

You can use the three communication styles with both invocation types, with one exception: you cannot use deferred synchronous communication with stub-style invocation. Most applications are likely to use some combination of these communication styles and invocation types.

## 8.2.1 Synchronous Communication

When an application invokes a synchronous communication request, the application transfers control to the ORB and cannot do anything until the request completes or fails. Synchronous communication is most appropriate when an application needs to send and complete requests in a certain order and the operations are of short duration. For example, such operations might be performed as a direct result of end-user input, such as displaying dialog boxes, opening files, or displaying directories. However, if you know how the server implements a request (because you have a specification or some other source of information), you can use synchronous communication for operations that are not time critical, such as a set of requests used in an overnight backup of data to tape.

If your vendor's CORBA system is thread-safe, you can invoke several synchronous stub-style requests simultaneously in different threads. No single request can prevent the others from running.

To use synchronous communication with stub-style invocation, you need to make sure that no operations in your interface definitions use the oneway attribute, indicating the one-way communication style. To use synchronous communication with dynamic invocation, you use the CORBA_Request_invoke operation.

## 8.2.2 Deferred Synchronous Communication

What CORBA refers to as the deferred synchronous communication style is a form of what the non-CORBA world calls asynchronous communication. When an application invokes a deferred synchronous request, the application does not wait for the request to complete before it continues with other work. However, the application must periodically check to see if the request has completed by polling using the CORBA_Request_get_response operation or the CORBA_get_next_response routine.

The deferred synchronous style of communication is most appropriate when you do not want your application to have to wait for the current request to complete before sending the next request. For example, if you do not know how long the operation may take, you may not want your application to wait for the request to complete. This will almost always be the case when you write a CORBA client to connect to someone else's framework or server.

CORBA supports deferred synchronous communication for dynamic invocation only. To use deferred synchronous communication, you use the CORBA_Request_send operation or the CORBA_send_multiple_requests routine to make a request.

## 8.2.3 One-Way Communication

When an application invokes a one-way request, the application sends the request and continues with other work without checking to see if the request is completed. The request truly goes only one way: the application sends the request to the server, but nothing is ever returned from it.

When you assign the oneway attribute to an operation in an interface definition, the sender will not be notified when requests are completed, there can be no return value, no output arguments, and only the ORB can raise exceptions. The semantics of one-way communication is that the ORB will only attempt to send the request once. Thus, although the sender cannot be sure that the request was delivered successfully, the request can return any of the standard exceptions to indicate the reason for the failure if the operation is not completed for some reason.

One-way communication is most appropriate for logging events that occur in your application and for notifying applications that an event has occurred, as long as no problems would arise if the log were incomplete or if some applications do not receive the notification. A more sophisticated use of the one-way communication style is as an event-driven communication mechanism for a client and server; for example, as part of a distributed system management tool. Suppose this tool consists of clients on each system that the tool manages and a server that runs on one system. As part of a logging activity, each managed client sends a one-way request to the system management server every 5 minutes. These requests contain information about the current state of the client system, such as the number of end users, the available disk space, and so on.

The server receives and stores the status information. If the server does not receive a request from a client, it takes no action because an occasional failure is expected, caused by networks being down and so on. However, if the server does not receive a client request within an hour, it queries the client using a synchronous or deferred synchronous request to see whether the client system is available on the network and whether the request was sent successfully.

Both stub-style and dynamic invocation support one-way communication. To use one-way communication, you invoke a request for an operation defined in OMG IDL with the oneway attribute. For example, Example 8–2 shows an OMG IDL code fragment with the oneway attribute assigned to the promote operation.

**Example 8–2  Use of the One-Way Attribute**

```
/* OMG IDL */

interface Employee
    {
    oneway void promote
        (in char new_job_class
        );
    }; //end interface Employee
```

If you are using dynamic deferred synchronous requests, you can also use the INV_NO_RESPONSE invocation request flag with the CORBA_Request_send operation or the CORBA_send_multiple_requests routine to indicate that the one-way communication style should be used, even if the operation you are requesting is not defined using the oneway attribute.

## 8.3 Choosing the Invocation Type

A client application can make requests only for operations on objects that it knows about. The application designer defines these operations and objects in the interface definitions stored in the OMG IDL file. How the client obtains these definitions is determined by how the request is invoked. CORBA provides two mechanisms for invoking requests:

- Stub-style invocation

- Dynamic invocation

Stub-style invocation is easier to use and may be faster than dynamic invocation, but stub-style is also less flexible. Figure 8–1 provides a conceptual look at both invocation types.

### 8.3.1 Stub-Style Invocation

When you use stub-style invocation, you are invoking a request that was constructed when the client stubs were compiled. These are the client stubs that you linked into your client application. When you use stub-style invocation, you are calling a stub procedure generated from your interface definitions that contains the information needed to request an operation on an object.

In the following sections, we'll take a look at some of the characteristics of stub-style invocation and go through a sample use of stub-style invocation using our personnel application framework as an example.

#### 8.3.1.1 Characteristics of Stub-Style Invocation

The major characteristics of stub-style invocation are as follows:

- Supports synchronous and one-way communication styles, but not deferred synchronous.

- Uses familiar routine-like calls.

  You perform a stub-style invocation using client stubs generated from your OMG IDL code. These client stubs are very similar to standard routine calls.

**Figure 8–1   Dynamic and Stub-Style Invocation**

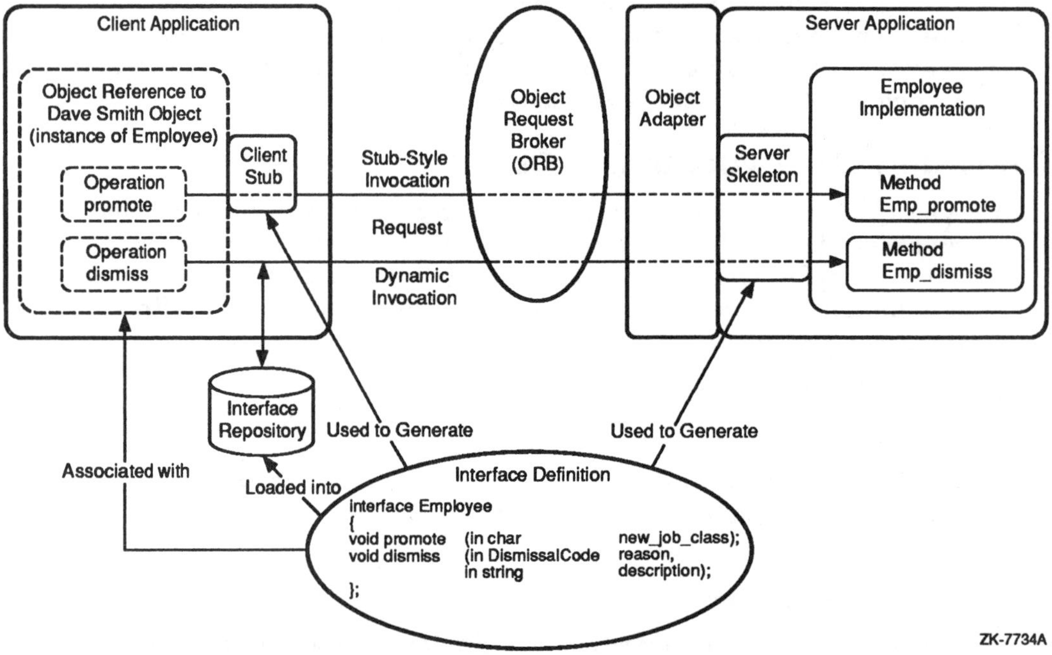

ZK-7734A

The header files and definitions produced when the OMG IDL file is compiled are, in turn, compiled into the client and placed in a hidden portion called a stub. A client stub is a set of local, language-specific procedures that map interface definitions to operations available on objects. When called, the stub supplies the signature of your object's operation to the request. To make a request, you call these client stubs from your client program in the same way that you would call a traditional programming language routine–you supply the required arguments and issue the call.

These routine-like calls are often more familiar to developers, and if so, may be easier to use than the object-oriented procedure a developer needs to handle when dynamically invoking a request. Stub-style invocation is very similar to using an RPC mechanism to communicate between a client and a server.

• Can be used only with interfaces that are completely known at the time the client stubs are compiled.

If you have a set of operations and objects that are completely defined when you compile your client stubs, then stub-style invocation might be a good choice for your client application. A client application that uses stub-style invocation must be deployed with client stubs for all the objects and operations it will use. If you want to add new objects or operations to a framework that will use stub-style invocation, you will need to add these interfaces, regenerate the client stubs, and redeploy all the affected clients with new stubs.

Stub-style invocation is best suited to data, objects, and operations that are relatively stable. For example, suppose the personnel application displays a menu of actions that an end user can perform on online personnel reports. To keep employee information confidential, the personnel department has limited this list to three well-defined actions that are unlikely to change. In this case, stub-style invocation would be a good choice.

If you need to be able to discover new interfaces that define new operations and objects for your application or framework without recompiling your applications, then you should use dynamic invocation.

* Might be faster than dynamic invocation.

Stub-style invocation uses client stubs generated from your interface definitions. These stubs contain information you need to make a stub-style invocation at run time. Since a dynamic invocation needs to, at the very least, perform some file input/output getting information from the interface repository, you might find that in some vendor's CORBA systems, stub-style invocation of a request takes less time than the dynamic invocation of the same request. This could be especially true if the interface repository that your client application needs to access is at a remote network location.

In general, whether stub-style invocation is faster than dynamic invocation depends greatly on how your vendor's CORBA system is built.

### 3.3.1.2 How to Use Stub-Style Invocation

Follow these steps to perform a stub-style invocation of a request:

1. Generate one or more client stubs from the interface definitions your client application will use.

   Generally, the stub will be an object or source file and will be connected to your client code by linking, or compiling and linking, the file in.

   Regardless of what form the client stub takes, you should just connect it and let it work. Each CORBA vendor will determine how the stub works. You should have no reason to look at the stub or to modify it in any way. If the stub needs modification for some reason, you should change your OMG IDL and regenerate the stub.

The following OMG IDL code is a modified portion of the interface definitions from the personnel application.

```
/* OMG IDL */

module CORP
{
.
.
.
interface Personnel
    {
    Employee hire
        (in    EmpData          employee_data,
         in    Department       department_obj,
         out   BadgeNum         new_employee_id)
        context(sec_level);
    }; // end of interface Personnel
.
.
.
}; //end of module CORP
```

The CORBA system on which the personnel application is being built has an OMG IDL compiler that accepts a file that contains the interface definitions as input, then generates client stubs in the C language for the client application. The compiler also generates a C include file (a .h file) that contains the function prototypes for the client stubs.

In the following example, the idl_compile command activates the OMG IDL compiler, the file CORP.idl contains the interface definitions, and the -c Personnel_client option indicates that the client stubs should have the filename of Personnel_client with the default file types.

```
> idl_compile  CORP.idl   -c Personnel_client
```

2. Connect the client stubs to your client applications.

You now need to compile and link the files generated in step 1 into the client applications. This mechanism is probably what most CORBA systems will use because it is familiar to most software developers. This part of the process will vary considerably across operating systems and tools.

The CORBA system used here generates C source files for the stubs. The following OMG IDL code shows the function prototype for the stub, which is placed in the C language Personnel_client.h file.

```
/* C */

CORBA_Object CORP_Personnel_hire
    (
    CORP_Personnel     object,
    CORBA_Environment * ev,
    CORBA_Context      * ctx_obj,
    CORP_EmpData       * employee_data,
    CORBA_Object       department_obj,
    CORP_BadgeNum      * new_employee_id
    );
```

3.  Get the references to the objects required for the request.

    In this example, we need to get the object references for specific instances
    of the Personnel, Context, and Department objects.

4.  Call the client stub from your client program, specifying the appropriate
    arguments.

    The following example shows the C call to the client stub from the client
    program. The arguments in the client stub correspond to those in the OMG
    IDL code fragment in step 2.

```
/* C */

new_emp_obj = CORP_Personnel_hire❶
    (
    personnel_obj ❷
    &Ev, ❸
    cxt_obj, ❹
    new_emp_data,❺
    dept_obj, ❻
    new_emp_badge❼
    );
```

❶ The variable new_emp_obj will be assigned the object reference
to the new instance of the employee object created with the
CORP_Personnel_hire operation. This corresponds to the Employee
object that is returned in the OMG IDL.

The vendor's stub generator creates unique client stub names according
to the CORBA specification, using the form:
modulename_interfacename_operationname. In this case, the client
stub CORP_Personnel_hire is for the hire operation on the Personnel
object, which is defined in the CORP module.

❷ The reference to the instance of the Personnel object on which the hire operation is defined, personnel_obj. This corresponds to the Personnel object in our OMG IDL definition. You will need to get this object reference by using the mechanism your CORBA vendor has provided.

❸ The address of the environment argument used to store exception information. This corresponds to nothing in our OMG IDL, but it is required for the C mapping of the OMG IDL definition.

❹ The reference to the context object associated with the request, using the variable cxt_obj. This corresponds to the context(sec_level) variable in our OMG IDL definition.

❺ The variable, new_emp_data, contains the employee data for the current object. This corresponds to the employee_data variable in the OMG IDL definition.

❻ The reference to the instance of the Department object that the employee is being hired into, dept_obj. This corresponds to the department_obj variable in the OMG IDL definition. Again, you will need to get this object reference in some way.

❼ The address of the argument to return a new employee badge number for the employee being hired, new_emp_badge. This corresponds to the new_employee_id variable in the OMG IDL definition. If the operation fails, the return value is undetermined.

5. Read the results from your stub call, if any, and use them. For example, the call returns a reference to the newly created employee object and that employee's badge number. End users can use this information to register the employee in the company's health and stock option plans.

6. Release the memory for any objects you own but no longer need.

If the operation in this example was defined with the oneway attribute, none of the arguments would have been able to be output arguments and nothing would have been returned. One-way behavior is not appropriate for this operation because its purpose is to create and return an employee object.

## 8.3.2 Dynamic Invocation

When you invoke a request using dynamic invocation, the request is fully constructed at run time using information from the interface repository, which is queried to retrieve the signature of the requested object's operations.

Dynamic invocation is best used when you want your client application to be able to discover new object types without having to redeploy the application. Dynamic invocation uses the interface repository to validate and possibly retrieve the signature of the operation on which you are making a request.

In the following sections, we'll take a look at some of the characteristics of dynamic invocation and go through a sample use of dynamic invocation using a part of our personnel application framework as an example. Appendix D briefly describes the dynamic invocation operations we discuss in this chapter. You may want to refer to these descriptions as you encounter these operations in the text.

### 8.3.2.1 Characteristics of Dynamic Invocation

The major characteristics of dynamic invocation are as follows:

- Supports synchronous, deferred synchronous, and one-way communication styles.

- Has a consistent, generalized object-oriented invocation model.

  When you use dynamic invocation, you always invoke a request in the same general way, doing things in the same order. Although dynamic invocation is a bit more complex to use than stub-style invocation, this generalized invocation model helps make it easier to use. This model consists of the following steps for dynamic invocation:

  1. Load the interface definitions into an interface repository.

  2. Get the object references needed for the request.

  3. Create a request object and add arguments to the request. Section 8.3.2.2 contains more information on adding arguments to the request.

  4. Invoke the request using synchronous, deferred synchronous, or one-way communications.

  5. Get the results, if any.

  6. Delete the request to conserve memory usage or keep portions of the request around if you plan to reuse it for another request.

  Section 8.3.2.3 contains more details on these steps.

- Allows run-time discovery of new kinds of objects and operations by applications and frameworks.

  This is done when the dynamic invocation accesses the interface repository at run time for information on the available objects and operations. For example, a CORBA application recently added to a framework could be discovered and made available at run time to the end user of a PC desktop.

  Dynamic invocation is best used for applications or frameworks in which the supported objects and operations might change after the client application is constructed. Because dynamic invocation can be used to discover supported operations and object interfaces at run time, the application might be able to dynamically integrate these new operations and object interfaces without requiring that all the client applications be redeployed, as would be the case for stub-style invocation.

- Might be slower than stub-style invocation.

  Because dynamically invoked requests need to access the interface repository, they might take longer to invoke than stub-style requests, especially if the interface repository is at a remote location from the client application. Whether dynamic invocation takes longer than stub-style invocation is very dependent on how your vendor's CORBA system is built.

### 8.3.2.2 Building Dynamically-Invoked Requests

Most of the work in using dynamic invocation lies in the building of the request, not the invocation itself. The actual invocation is as simple as performing a stub-style invocation.

A request consists of three parts:

- Object reference
- Operations
- Arguments

There are three ways to complete these three parts in a dynamic request:

- Automatically, using the `CORBA_ORB_create_operation_list` operation

  This is the easiest way, but has the poorest performance of the three methods. With this method, you need to do the following:

  - Create a named value list and populate it with the name and data type of the arguments, but no argument values. A named value list is a CORBA-defined structure that contains a name, a data type, a length, any associated flags, and the order of all the arguments used by your operation.

- Set the values for the arguments.
- Create the request object specifying the object reference, operation name, and named value list.

• Adding arguments to the request object one at a time, using the CORBA_Request_add_arg operation

With this method, you need to do the following:

- Create the request object specifying the object reference, operation name, but no arguments.
- Specify the name, data type, and value for each argument one at a time.

• Manually, using the CORBA_ORB_create_list operation

With this method, you need to do the following:

- Create a named value list with NULL arguments.
- Manually populate the list with the name, data type, and value for the arguments.
- Create the request object specifying the object reference, operation name, and named value list.

The following sections describe these three methods in greater detail.

### Building the Request Automatically

The simplest way to build a dynamic request is to do so automatically, using the CORBA_ORB_create_operation_list operation; this lets the ORB automate most of the work of building the operation list. Having the ORB build the list also makes the request more likely to be error free because no other data is provided manually.

To build the request automatically, do the following:

1. Use the CORBA_ORB_create_operation_list operation to build an operation argument list.

   This operation creates a named value list. The following example shows how to use the CORBA_ORB_create_operation_list operation to build an operation argument list for our CORP_Personnel_hire operation.

```
/* C */
status = CORBA_ORB_create_operation_list
    (
    ORB_obj, ❶
    &Ev, ❷
    hire_opdef_obj, ❸
    &hire_op_NVList ❹
    );
```

❶ The object reference. The first argument you need to supply is a reference to the ORB object because this operation is defined on that object. In this example, the reference to the ORB object is placed in the variable ORB_obj.

The method for getting object references will vary depending on your CORBA vendor.

❷ The address of the environment argument.

❸ A reference to the OperationDef object for a particular operation on a particular interface. The OperationDef object is used in the interface repository to represent such operations.

When used with the CORBA_ORB_create_operation_list operation, an OperationDef object represents the operation you want to request, This object provides the information the CORBA_ORB_create_operation_list operation needs to create the named value list with the appropriate number and types of arguments for the operation you want to request.

In this example, the reference to the OperationDef object represents the information about the CORP_Personnel_hire operation that is stored in the interface repository; the variable hire_opdef_obj holds this information. More information about using the interface repository is provided in Chapter 8.

❹ The address of a named value list. This argument will receive the named value list that contains the arguments for the operation you want to request, but without any values associated with those arguments. The CORBA_ORB_create_operation_list builds this list operation using the argument information retrieved from the interface definitions stored in the interface repository, which was accessed using the OperationDef object.

In the example, the variable associated with the named value list is hire_op_NVList.

2. Assign appropriate values for in arguments, buffers to receive out arguments, and buffers initialized with values for inout arguments.

   At this point, you know what the arguments are supposed to be (name, data type, value, and so on), so you can set them in the named value list array.

3. Create a request object using the CORBA_Object_create_request operation and specify the named value list created in step 1.

   The following example shows a C language code fragment of a client program that illustrates how to use the CORBA_Object_create_request operation to build a request for the CORP_Personnel_hire operation.

```c
/* C */
status = CORBA_Object_create_request
    (
    personnel_obj,  ❶
    &Ev,  ❷
    "hire",  ❸
    hire_op_NVList,  ❹
    emp_obj,  ❺
    &req_obj,  ❻
    0  ❼
    );
```

❶ The object reference. To request an operation defined on the Personnel object, the object reference is supplied in the variable personnel_obj.

❷ The address of the environment argument.

❸ A string that contains the name of the operation to be invoked. In this case, it is the hire operation on the Personnel object, so the string name is hire. It is not necessary to use the fully scoped operation name, CORP_Personnel_hire, because the scope is already established.

❹ The named value list argument, hire_op_NVList, created previously with the CORBA_ORB_create_operation_list operation.

❺ A placeholder for the results of the request, if any. If there are no results, this argument should be NULL.

   In this example, the request for the hire operation returns an object reference to an Employee object, which is placed in the variable emp_obj.

❻ The address of the object reference for the request object being created. In this example, the variable &req_obj contains the address of the reference to the request object created by this operation.

❼ The argument used to pass flags to CORBA that affect the creation of a request object. CORBA currently defines only a single flag, OUT_LIST_MEMORY, on the CORBA_Object_create_request operation for managing memory associated with lists. This flag is not used in this example; a value of 0 indicates that no flag is being passed.

**Adding Arguments to the Request Object One at a Time**

If you do not know the values to all arguments when you build the request, you can use the CORBA_Request_add_arg operation to add them. This operation lets you add arguments and their values to a request one at a time.

A good way to use this operation would be to build a request as input is received from an end user who is filling in fields in a dialog box; the number of arguments and the data types for each are known, but the values cannot be known until the end user fills in the fields.

To add values to arguments manually, do the following:

1. Create a request object using the CORBA_Object_create_request and specify the argument named value list as NULL.

   In the example, the argument hire_op_NVList would be replaced by NULL to indicate that the request will contain an embedded argument list.

2. Assign appropriate values for in arguments, buffers to receive out arguments, and buffers initialized with values for inout arguments.

   At this point, you know what the arguments are supposed to be (name, data type, value, and so on), so you can set them in the named value list array.

**Building the Request Manually**

Building a request manually is not recommended because it is more prone to introducing errors. However, there might be some reason to use this operation to build a request, depending on your CORBA vendor's system.

To build a request manually, do the following:

1. Create a named value list using the CORBA_ORB_create_list operation.

2. Assign appropriate values for in arguments, buffers to receive out arguments, and buffers initialized with values for inout arguments.

   At this point, you know what the arguments are supposed to be (name, data type, value, and so on), so you can set them in the named value list array.

3. Create a request object with the CORBA_Object_create_request operation, then pass in the named value list as the operation argument list to the request object.

### 8.3.2.3 How to Use Dynamic Invocation

In this section, we use the OMG IDL code fragment from Section 8.3.1.2 to illustrate how to use dynamic invocation. Follow these steps to perform a dynamic invocation of a request:

1. Load your interface definitions into an interface repository. In this example, the CORBA system has provided the idl_load command as the mechanism for loading the interface definitions.

   ```
   > idl_load CORP.idl
   ```

2. Get the object references for the objects you need for the request.

   In this example, the object references for specific instances of the Personnel, Context, and Department objects are needed.

3. Build the request.

   Use one of the three techniques for building the request as described in Section 8.3.2.2.

4. Invoke the request.

   Now that the request is completely filled in, you can invoke the request in one of several ways:

   - Make a synchronous invocation using the CORBA_Request_invoke operation.

   - Make a deferred synchronous invocation using the CORBA_Request_send operation.

   - Make a multiple deferred synchronous invocation using the CORBA_send_multiple_requests routine.

   You use these three operations in a similar fashion. The following example uses synchronous invocation. Note that it provides no error handling.

   ```
   /* C */
   status = CORBA_Request_invoke
       (
       req_obj,  ❶
       &Ev,  ❷
       0 ❸
       );
   ```

❶ A reference to the request object. This example specifies the reference to the request object built previously and stored in the variable `req_obj`.

❷ The address of the environment argument.

❸ The final argument allows you to specify any flags that can be defined on the invocation. The example uses the `CORBA_Request_invoke` operation, which has no flags defined for it. You specify this value as `0` to indicate that there are no flags defined.

5. Get the results, if any.

   If you are using deferred synchronous and synchronous communication, CORBA passes the results back in the named value list stored in the request object. You need to read the values from that list. If you are using one-way communication, there are no results to retrieve because no results can be returned.

6. Reinvoke the request, or delete it and issue another one.

   It is possible to reuse components of a previous request. Once you have been notified that the request is successfully completed, you must decide how much of the request to use in the next invocation. This decision tends to result in two choices:

   • Reinvoke the request with the named value list that contains the same argument list.

     To reinvoke a dynamic request with the same named value list, use the `CORBA_NVList_free_memory` operation on the `CORBA_NVList` object to free the memory associated with the output arguments in an argument list. For more information, see Section 8.3.2.4.

   • Delete this request and issue another one.

     To delete the entire request, use the `CORBA_Request_delete` operation on the request object to be deleted. This operation releases all memory associated with the request.

     Note that deleting a request that was issued using the deferred synchronous communication style can cause that request to be canceled. This behavior depends largely on your vendor's CORBA system.

### 8.3.2.4 Memory Management

To free the memory associated with the output arguments in an argument list, use the CORBA_NVList_free_memory operation on the CORBA_NVList object. By doing this, you create an argument list that is the same as one created using the CORBA_ORB_create_operation_list operation, except that all of the input arguments entered previously are retained.

To use the CORBA_NVList_free_memory operation to free the memory associated with the output arguments in a named value argument list, you must set the OUT_LIST_MEMORY flag to the CORBA_Object_create_request operation. When you use this flag, all memory associated with your output arguments is assigned to your CORBA_NVList object. When the CORBA_NVList object has its memory freed using the CORBA_NVList_free_memory operation, all of the output arguments are freed as well. If the OUT_LIST_MEMORY flag is not set on the CORBA_Object_create_request operation, each output argument must be freed individually.

# 8.4 General Process of Building a CORBA Client Application

We are now ready to look at how to develop the client side of a CORBA application. Remember that, in CORBA, an application can be a client, a server, or most often, both. We'll discuss how to develop the client side of a CORBA application by first looking at portions of a simple client program and then looking at topics associated with building a more complex client program.

Whether your client is simple or complex, you will perform the following general steps in developing that client:

1. Design and write the non-CORBA portions of your code, based on what functions you need to provide to your end users, what user interface you will provide, and so on.

2. Choose the communication styles (synchronous, deferred synchronous, or one-way) and invocation types (stub-style invocation, dynamic invocation, or both) that you will need to support your application's capabilities as discussed at the beginning of this chapter.

3. Support the invocation types you have chosen by making available the interface definitions the client needs to invoke requests.

   How you support the invocation type varies:

   • If your client code supports only stub-style invocation, generate your client stubs from the OMG IDL code and connect them to your client application.

- If your client code supports only dynamic invocation, load your OMG IDL code into the interface repository.

- If your client code supports both stub-style and dynamic invocation, do the tasks described in the two previous list items.

4. Write the client application code that actually invokes the requests you use and gets the information you need to do the invocations, such as getting the appropriate object references and other arguments.

5. Write the client application code to receive the results or returns of a successful request.

6. Write the client application code to handle any user-defined or standard exception (error) that is returned indicating a problem with the request.

7. If this application can also act as a server, perform the additional tasks discussed in Chapter 9.

## 8.5 Developing a Simple Client Application

In this section we'll develop a client application. To keep it simple so that we can focus on the basics of writing a CORBA client, our client application will have the following characteristics:

- We'll assume that all the non-CORBA aspects of the client application have been designed and that this application meets the needs of its end users.

- The client application will use only stub-style invocation, so we will link in client stubs but we won't need to use any of the CORBA operations associated with building a request for dynamic invocation.

- The client application will send a request for only a single operation on a single type of object.

- The client application will use minimal error and exception handling.

- The client application will not use the context object.

Section 8.7 shows the complete C source code for the simple client application with annotations to explain the code. We will be showing parts of the source code for this program as we discuss developing the simple client application. We will also show variations on this source code to introduce other topics associated with developing a client application that are not covered in the sample client application. Appendix A repeats the C source code for the sample client application without the annotations for you to use as a quick reference and also includes C++ source code for the sample client application.

## 8.5.1 Supporting Stub-Style Invocation

We discussed how to do stub-style invocation at the beginning of this chapter. In this section, we quickly review the process in the context of developing a client.

Because the simple client application uses stub-style invocation, we generate client stubs from the interface definitions on which the client will be invoking requests. CORBA vendors let you generate your client stubs from the interface repository, from an OMG IDL compiler, or from either if both are provided.

Once generated, we connect the client stubs to the client application. Most CORBA vendors generate their client stubs as source code, so to connect them you need to compile the client stubs and then link them to the client application.

Example 8–3 shows an annotated example of client stubs being generated, compiled, and then linked into a client program on a UNIX system—the exact syntax and commands used will vary with your operating system and CORBA vendor.

**Example 8–3  Generating and Connecting Client Stubs**

```
> ls ❶
CORP.idl          client_main.c     client_main.o
>

> idl_compile  -c CORP_cstub.c CORP.idl ❷
> ls
client_main.c     client_main.o     CORP.h
CORP.idl          CORP_cstub.c
>

>cc -c CORP_cstub.c ❸
>ls
client_main.c     client_main.o     CORP.h
CORP.idl          CORP_cstub.c      CORP_cstub.o
>

>cc -o client_main CORP_main.o CORP_cstubs.o -l ORB ❹
>ls
client_main       client_main.c     client_main.o
CORP.idl          CORP.h            CORP_cstub.c
CORP_cstub.o
>
```

❶ The ls command is a UNIX command for listing the contents of a directory. The following lines display the files in the directory:

> CORP.idl, the OMG IDL source file
> client_main.c, the main client application source file
> client_main.o, the main client application object file

❷ This line shows the idl_compile command being used to activate the example OMG IDL compiler. Here, the OMG IDL source file, CORP.idl, is specified as input and the -c CORP_cstub.c option indicates that a client stub with that name should be created.

As a result, this compiler generates the client stub file CORP_cstub.c and also a C header file CORP.h.

❸ This line shows the client stub, CORP_cstub.c, being compiled by the C compiler, resulting in the object file CORP_cstub.o.

❹ This line shows the executable file, client_main, being created by linking together the client stub object file CORP_cstub.o, the main client application object file client_main.o, and the CORBA vendor's ORB library ORB which contains the definitions for the CORBA routines.

Now that we know how to create client stubs and connect them to our client application, let's take a closer look at what exactly a client stub is in CORBA.

## 8.5.2 A Closer Look at Client Stubs

Client stubs provide the definitions and other CORBA vendor-specific information you need to use stub-style invocation in your client application. The client stubs map OMG IDL operation definitions for an object type (defined by an interface definition) into procedural routines that applications will call to invoke a request. Although most vendors will generate your client stubs in source code format, you should treat them as a black box that you compile and link in, because some of the information in the client stubs is private to, and subject to change by, the CORBA vendor.

this line ind To better understand client stubs and their relationship to the interface definitions they are generated from, let's compare the signature of some operations defined as part of an interface and the signature of the client stubs generated from those operations.

Example 8–4 shows an annotated side-by-side comparison of the signature of the promote and dismiss operations defined in OMG IDL and the signatures of the C language client stubs generated from those operations.

**Example 8–4  Comparing the Signatures of Two OMG IDL Operations and Their Generated Client Stubs**

```
OMG IDL Operation Signature        | Generated C Client Stub Signature
---------------------------        | ----------------------------------
/* OMG IDL */                      | /* C */
                                   |
module CORP                        |
{                                  |
enum DismissalCode                 |
  { DISMISS_FIRED,                 |
    DISMISS_QUIT};                 |
interface Employee                 |
  {                                |
  void promote                     | void CORP_Employee_promote    ❶
     (                             |    (
                                   |    CORP_Employee      object,  ❷
                                   |    CORBA_Environment * ev,      ❸
      in char        new_job_class | CORBA_char        new_job_class ❶
      );                           |    );
                                   |
  void dismiss                     | void CORP_Employee_dismiss
     (                             |    (
                                   |    CORP_Employee      object,
                                   |    CORBA_Environment * ev,
      in DismissalCode reason,     | CORP_DismissalCode reason,
      in string       description  | CORBA_string       description
      );                           |    );
  }; // end of interface Employee  |
}; //end of module CORP            |
```

❶ This line indicates how the OMG IDL-defined promote operation on the Employee interface in the CORP module is generated as the C client stub name CORP_Employee_promote.

CORBA specifies that C client stubs should be named so that they are unique. The following is how a C client stub name is generated:

1. A client stub name begins with the name (if any) of the OMG IDL module in which the operation was defined, in this example, CORP, and is followed by an underscore character (_). If multiple modules are nested, each module name is prepended followed by an underscore that separates each module name. The case of the module is kept as specified in OMG IDL.

2. The name of the interface containing the operation, in this example, Employee, follows the underscore and is itself followed by an underscore character. The case of the interface is kept as specified in OMG IDL.

3. The name of the operation, in this example, promote or dismiss, follows the underscore and ends the name of the client stub. The case of the operation is kept as specified in OMG IDL.

❷ This line indicates the object reference needed to complete the request that will be sent using stub-style invocation. In this example, it would be the object reference for the specific employee who is being promoted. Note that the data type CORP_Employee is prefixed by the name of the module in which it was defined, in this example, CORP.IDL.

❸ This line indicates the address of the environment argument used to hold status information for this request. In this example, it is the argument named ev.

❹ This line indicates how the OMG IDL data type, char, is generated into a C data type named CORBA_char.

When you map CORBA's OMG IDL to programming languages, all names and keywords that CORBA defines are treated as if they were defined in an OMG IDL module named CORBA. So, in this example, the OMG IDL char data type is generated as a C data type named CORBA_char.

In addition, this line shows the OMG IDL direction attribute, in. This attribute is used to determine how the argument will be passed between the client and the server. In most cases in C, a direction attribute of in will be passed by value, as in this example, with new_job_class. If new_job_class had a direction attribute that allowed it to be modified by the server, such as inout or out, then it would have been passed by reference as *new_job_class.

## 8.5.3 Formatting a Request

The general form of a request is the same for both dynamic and stub-style invocation. A request consists of an operation, a reference to the object on which that operation is defined, a reference to a context object (optional), and zero or more additional arguments specific to the operation being requested.

The way a client application invokes a request differs depending on whether the client application is using stub-style invocation or dynamic invocation. In our example client application, we show only stub-style invocation.

Example 8–5 shows a stub-style request for the promote operation to be performed on an Employee object. The example shows a variation on the stub-style request in our sample application. In our sample client application, we do not use the context object because it was not defined as part of any of the interfaces we invoke; however, the following example uses the context object so you can see where it fits into a request. When the context object is part of a request, it is always the third argument in that request for C language bindings.

**Example 8–5  Formatting a Stub-Style Request**

```
/* C */
void CORP_Employee_promote
(
CORP_Employee      object,        ❶
CORBA_Environment *ev,            ❷
CORBA_Context      cxt_obj,       ❸
CORBA_char         new_job_class  ❹
);
```

❶  This line indicates the object argument. This argument is the object reference to the specific employee object that is to have the promote operation performed on it.

❷  This line indicates the ev argument. This argument is the contents of the environment argument that can contain exception information from the request.

❸  This line indicates the cxt_obj argument. This argument is the object reference to the specific context object associated with this request. The context object may or may not be defined as part of an operation in an interface definition, so it may not appear in the client stub for a given operation.

❹  This line indicates the new_job_class argument. This argument is specific to this particular request and is a single character denoting the job classification of the employee being promoted.

## 8.5.4  Getting the Results of a Request

When a request is completed, you get the results from a request in the same manner for both dynamic and stub-style invocation. In fact, getting the results of a request is very similar to getting the results from a function in a programming language.

Any information that the operation was supposed to return, either as a result or as an output argument, is placed into the memory set up for that information. For example, if, in the previous example of the CORP_Employee_promote routine, the new_job_class argument were an output argument, then the character that represented the new job classification would be placed into the memory associated with that variable.

### 8.5.5 Getting Object References for a Request

To invoke a request, a client application first needs to get an object reference on which to make that request. Client applications generally get object references by invoking a request; however, because a request requires an object reference as an argument in the first place, this obviously won't work for the first few object references the client needs. To solve this problem, each CORBA vendor needs to supply a way for a client to obtain its first few object references so that the client can begin to invoke requests.

The client application can only obtain the object references it needs through the mechanisms the framework or server writer has provided. How the framework or server provides object references to the client varies, depending on the capabilities of the CORBA vendor or framework. For example, the server or framework could generate and store the object references as strings in a file or store them using some kind of registry or name service. The client could then obtain its object references by reading the external file in which the object references are stored. The most portable way for your server to publish object references and for your client to retrieve them is to use the naming service described in the OMG *Common Object Services Specification, Volume I*, if your CORBA vendor supports the naming service.

For simplicity, our client application reads an external file that was populated by a server to get its object references. In the client application, the first object references we get are to instances of the personnel object. We get these object references from an external file and pass them as arguments in the request to hire an employee object. The hire operation then creates an employee and returns an object reference to that employee. We are now free to perform other requests on the new employee object.

Example 8–6 is annotated and shows our client application getting the personnel object reference from a file.

**Example 8–6  Getting an Object Reference From a File**

```c
/* C */
/* Get the Personnel object reference from the file */
temp_file = fopen("PersFile.dat", "r");  ❶
if (temp_file == NULL)
    {
     fprintf(stderr,"Could not open file to get Personnel object reference\n");
     exit(0);
    }
if (fgets(string_obj, sizeof(string_obj), temp_file) == NULL)
    {
     fprintf(stderr,"Could not read the Personnel object reference from the file\n");
     exit(0);
    }
fclose(temp_file);

/* Convert the string-formatted Personnel object reference to a binary-formatted
   object reference */

pers_obj = CORBA_ORB_string_to_object(  ❷
                          CORBA_Vendor_ORB_OBJECT,  ❸
                          & ev,
                          string_obj
                          );
exit;
```

❶ This line shows the file PersFile.dat being opened. The following lines show the file having a personnel object reference in string format read from the file.

❷ This line and the following lines show the string-formatted Personnel object reference being converted to a binary-formatted object reference by using the CORBA_ORB_string_to_object routine.

❸ This line shows that the first argument to the CORBA_ORB_string_to_object routine is an object reference to the ORB itself, in this example, CORBA_Vendor_ORB_OBJECT. Because each CORBA vendor has a different ORB, we are using the name CORBA_Vendor_ORB_OBJECT to indicate a particular vendor's ORB in this example.

## 8.5.6 Handling Errors and Exceptions

Now that you know how a request works, we need to discuss how to handle any errors that might be signaled as a result of the request being processed. There are two mechanisms specified in CORBA for signaling errors:

- The CORBA_Status variable that is associated with some CORBA operations (mostly those operations used for dynamic invocation).

- Exceptions raised and stored in the environment argument to the request.

If you do not want your client to be too dependent on any particular CORBA vendor, you should not use the CORBA_Status variable because the information on how to define this variable and how it works is vendor-specific. According to CORBA, a CORBA vendor can assign the CORBA_Status variable a data type of either unsigned long or void. And if the data type of the variable is an unsigned long that you can look at, CORBA does not specify what status values are defined for the CORBA_Status variable, such as what value corresponds to a success or failure. However, if your CORBA vendor supports the use of CORBA_Status as an error handling mechanism, you might have vendor-specific reasons to use it.

The most well-defined (and therefore most portable between CORBA vendors) method of handling errors in CORBA is through the use of exceptions stored in, and retrieved from, the environment argument to the request. An exception is raised when an operation request is not performed successfully. The exception might be accompanied by additional, exception-specific information stored in a specialized record format.

Exceptions are defined in the CORBA system and can also be defined in your interface definitions. Either the ORB or the implementation can raise (signal) exceptions and the client can respond to them.

As explained previously in Section 7.4, there are two kinds of exceptions:

- Standard exceptions

  Can be raised by the ORB or by the implementation. Standard exceptions can apply to any request and, therefore, are fairly generic. For example, BAD_PARAM and NO_MEMORY are examples of standard exceptions. Table C–1 lists the standard exceptions.

- User-defined exceptions

  Can be raised only by the implementation. User-defined exceptions are defined in the interface definitions by using the exception statement and are made part of an interface by using the raises clause. For example, HIRING_FREEZE and NO_SUCH_DEPT are examples of user-defined exceptions that the hire operation can raise.

User-defined exceptions are known to both the client and the
implementation because both the client and implementation support
the same interface for the operation in which the user-defined exception is
defined.

Client applications should always check for standard exceptions, because
they can be raised on any request that is invoked. If a client application
uses a request that has user-defined exceptions defined on it, then the client
application should check for user-defined exceptions as well.

### 8.5.6.1 Determining the Type of Exception Returned

To determine whether an exception was returned and, if it was returned,
what kind of exception it is, you can check the contents of the environment
argument in the request. CORBA defines the environment argument as a
partially opaque structure whose data type is CORBA_Environment and which
contains at least one member named _major. Example 8–7 shows this partial
C declaration of the environment argument:

**Example 8–7  Declaration of the Environment Argument**

```
/* C */

typedef struct CORBA_Environment
    {
    CORBA_exception_type _major;
    .
    .
    .
    } CORBA_Environment;
```

When an invocation of a request is completed and the results, if any, are
returned, the _major member of the CORBA_Environment struct indicates
whether the invocation was completed successfully. The _major member can
have any of the values listed in Table 8–3.

**Table 8–3 Values for the** `_major` **Member**

| Value of `_major` Member | Description |
|---|---|
| CORBA_NO_EXCEPTION | Indicates that no exception occurred and that the invocation was completed successfully. |
| CORBA_SYSTEM_EXCEPTION | Indicates that the invocation was unsuccessful in some way and that a system-defined exception (standard exception) is available. |
| CORBA_USER_EXCEPTION | Indicates that the invocation was unsuccessful in some way and that a user-defined exception is available. |

If the value of the `_major` member is CORBA_NO_EXCEPTION, there is no exception to be handled; otherwise, you need to access the environment argument further to get the standard or user-defined exception.

### 8.5.6.2 Accessing Exception Information in the Environment Argument

You can access the exception information in the environment argument by using the following C routines that are defined as part of CORBA's C mapping. These routines allow you to get the character string that identifies the exception, to get a pointer to the structure associated with the exception, and to free the exception when you are finished with it.

- `CORBA_exception_id`

  Returns a pointer to the character-string literal that identifies the exception. This character-string literal is defined by the CORBA system for standard exceptions and for user-defined exceptions generated from the exception definition in the interface definition. If this routine is used on an environment argument that has no exception information (the `_major` member has the value CORBA_NO_EXCEPTION), the routine returns a NULL value.

  The C signature for this routine is as follows:

  ```
  CORBA_char *CORBA_exception_id(CORBA_Environment *ev);
  ```

- `CORBA_exception_value`

  Returns a pointer to the structure associated with the exception. If this routine is used on an environment argument that has no exception information, the routine returns a NULL value.

  The C signature for this routine is as follows:

  ```
  void *CORBA_exception_value(CORBA_Environment *ev);
  ```

- CORBA_exception_free

  Frees any storage allocated in the construction of the environment argument. This routine can be used on an environment argument regardless of whether there is exception information in the environment argument.

  The C signature for this routine is as follows:

  ```
  void  CORBA_exception_free(CORBA_Environment *ev);
  ```

Although you use these routines for both standard and user-defined exceptions, the structures used by standard and user-defined exceptions differ and need to be handled differently.

### 8.5.6.3 Handling User-Defined Exceptions

You define the body of a user-defined exception in your OMG IDL code as discussed in Chapter 4. For example, Example 8–8 shows the OMG IDL code for defining the exceptions HIRING_FREEZE and NO_SUCH_DEPT, and allows them to be raised as the result of a request for the hire operation on an instance of the Personnel object.

**Example 8–8  User-Defined Exceptions (OMG IDL Code)**

```
/* CORP.IDL */
module CORP
{
/* Define user-defined exceptions before using them */
exception HIRING_FREEZE
    {
    unsigned long      reason;
    };
exception NO_SUCH_DEPT
    {
    unsigned long      reason;
    };
```

(continued on next page)

### Example 8–8 (Cont.)  User-Defined Exceptions (OMG IDL Code)

```
/* Define Personnel interface */

interface Personnel : Employee
    {
    Employee hire (in  EmpData      employee_data,
                   in  Department   department_obj,
                   out BadgeNum     new_employee_id)
                   raises (HIRING_FREEZE, NO_SUCH_DEPT);
    };// end of interface Personnel

}; //end of module CORP
```

The previous OMG IDL code for the HIRING_FREEZE and NO_SUCH_DEPT
exceptions would result in something like the C code being generated as shown
in Example 8–9. In this code, the exceptions are first defined as string literals,
then the exceptions themselves are mapped to C structure data types. Each
structure contains a single member whose data type is an unsigned long, which
indicates the reason for the exception being raised. This number can then be
mapped to a listing of error codes known to the client.

### Example 8–9  User-Defined Exceptions (C Code)

```
/* C */

#define ex_CORP_HIRING_FREEZE "1000001"
#define ex_CORP_NO_SUCH_DEPT  "1000002"

typedef struct CORP_HIRING_FREEZE
    {
    CORBA_unsigned_long reason;
    }CORP_HIRING_FREEZE;

typedef struct CORP_NO_SUCH_DEPT
    {
    CORBA_unsigned_long reason;
    }CORP_NO_SUCH_DEPT;
```

Now that we know how exceptions are defined in C, we can discuss the process
needed to access the information in those exceptions:

1.  Check the _major member of the environment argument to the request
    to determine the kind of exception. In this example, it is a user-defined
    exception because the value of _major is CORBA_USER_EXCEPTION.

2. Use the CORBA_exception_id routine to get the exception identifier for the user-defined exception and match it against all the defined user exceptions to determine which exception is associated with this request.

3. Use the CORBA_exception_value routine to get a pointer to the structure associated with the exception.

4. Read the values of whatever members are part of the user-defined exception structure to get additional information about the exception. In our example, there is a single reason member in the user-defined exception that contains that exception information.

5. Use the information gained from the preceding steps to determine what your application should do next. You should be aware that, when an exception is raised, any output arguments associated with the request should be considered invalid and not be used.

6. Free the memory associated with the environment argument by using the CORBA_exception_free routine.

For an example of user-defined exception handling, see Example 8–12 in Section 8.5.6.4.

### 8.5.6.4 Handling Standard Exceptions

Standard exceptions are like user-defined exceptions, except that CORBA defines the structures associated with them. CORBA defines a standard exception body as having two parts: minor whose data type is an unsigned long and completed whose data type is an enumerated type. Table 8–4 summarizes what we said about these parts of the exception in Chapter 4.

**Table 8–4  Parts of a Standard Exception**

| Exception Part | Description |
|---|---|
| minor | The value of minor indicates the subcategory of the exception. CORBA has not standardized these values; therefore, they will vary among vendors. |
| completed | The value of completed lets the client application determine when in the request process the exception was signaled. A value of CORBA_COMPLETED_YES indicates the exception was raised after the implementation had completed. |

(continued on next page)

**Table 8–4 (Cont.)  Parts of a Standard Exception**

| Exception Part | Description |
| --- | --- |
| | A value of CORBA_COMPLETED_NO indicates the exception was raised before the implementation was initiated, and therefore, the implementation was not initiated by the request. A value of CORBA_COMPLETED_MAYBE indicates the exception was raised when the state of the implementation was not determined. |

Although we previously showed the OMG IDL defining a user-defined exception, this is difficult to do with standard exceptions because standard exceptions are defined within a vendor's CORBA system, so the OMG IDL might not be available to the software developer. However, Example 8–10 shows the most likely OMG IDL definition for a standard exception in a portion of the CORBA system that is part of the module CORBA.IDL. In this example, the UNKNOWN standard exception is defined, although all the standard exceptions would have the same form.

**Example 8–10  Defining Standard Exceptions (OMG IDL Code)**

```
/* OMG IDL */

module CORBA
{
enum completion_status { COMPLETED_YES, COMPLETED_NO, COMPLETED_MAYBE};

/* Define UNKNOWN standard exception */

exception UNKNOWN
    {
    unsigned long     minor;
    completion_status completed;
    };
};
```

The OMG IDL definition shown in Example 8–10 for the UNKNOWN exception would result in the C code being generated as shown in Example 8–11. In this example, the OMG IDL exception name is first associated with a unique string literal identifier. The exception itself is then mapped to a C structure with a minor member and a completed member.

**Example 8–11  Defining Standard Exceptions (C Code)**

```c
/* C */

typedef unsigned long CORBA_enum;
typedef unsigned long CORBA_completion_status;

#define CORBA_COMPLETED_YES    (CORBA_completion_status) 0;
#define CORBA_COMPLETED_NO     (CORBA_completion_status) 1;
#define CORBA_COMPLETED_MAYBE  (CORBA_completion_status) 2;

/* Define UNKNOWN standard exception */

#define EX_CORBA_UNKNOWN '1001233';

typedef struct CORBA_UNKNOWN
    {
    CORBA_unsigned_long minor;
    CORBA_completion_status completed;
    } CORBA_UNKNOWN;
```

Now that we know the form of a standard exception defined in C, we can discuss the process we need to use to access the information in that standard exception:

1. Check the _major member of the environment argument to the request to determine the kind of exception. In this example, it is a standard exception because the value of _major is CORBA_SYSTEM_EXCEPTION.

2. Use the CORBA_exception_id routine to get the exception identifier for the standard exception and match it against all the defined standard exceptions to determine which exception is associated with this request. Table C–1 in Appendix C lists the standard exceptions.

3. Use the CORBA_exception_value routine to get a pointer to the structure associated with the exception.

4. Read the value of the minor member of the exception structure to get additional information about the exception.

   Because CORBA does not define the values of the minor member, the values will be vendor specific and will need to be handled and interpreted as your CORBA vendor indicates.

5. Read the value of the completed member of the exception to determine which of the three completion types was recorded.

6. Use the information gained from the preceding steps to determine what your application should do next. You should be aware that when an exception is raised, any output arguments associated with the request should be considered invalid and not be used.

7.  Free the memory associated with the environment argument by using the
    CORBA_exception_free routine.

Example 8–12 shows an annotated portion of a C client application that
handles both standard and user-defined exceptions. This code would probably
occur in a C macro and be called after each invocation of a request to handle
exception information that was returned by the request.

**Example 8–12  Sample Client Code to Handle Exceptions**

```
/* C */
CORBA_void * cur_ex_value; ❶
/* Check for and process all exceptions */
switch(ev._major) ❷
    {
    /* If there is no exception, success */
    case CORBA_NO_EXCEPTION: ❸
        break;

    /* If there is a user-defined exception, check each one for a match */
    case CORBA_USER_EXCEPTION: ❹

        /* If the user-defined exception is HIRING_FREEZE */
        if (strcmp (ex_CORP_HIRING_FREEZE, CORBA_exception_id(&ev) ) == 0 ❺
            {
            /* Retrieve and print the value associated with this failure */
            cur_ex_value = CORBA_exception_value(&ev); ❻
            fprintf(stderr, ❼
                    "Failure code is: %d\n",
                    (CORP_HIRING_FREEZE *)cur_ex_value->reason
                    );
            }
        else
            /* If the user-defined exception is NO_SUCH_DEPT */
            if (strcmp (ex_CORP_NO_SUCH_DEPT, CORBA_exception_id(&ev) ) == 0
                {
                /* Retrieve and print the value associated with this failure */
                cur_ex_value = CORBA_exception_value(&ev);
                fprintf(stderr,
                        "Failure code is: %d\n",
                        (CORP_NO_SUCH_DEPT *)cur_ex_value->reason
                        );
                }
```

(continued on next page)

**Example 8–12 (Cont.)  Sample Client Code to Handle Exceptions**

```
                else
                    {
                    /* unrecognized user-defined exception */
                    fprintf(stderr,
                            "Internal Error--Unrecognized User Exception\n"
                            );
                    }
        break;

        /* If there is a standard exception, check each one for a match */
        case CORBA_SYSTEM_EXCEPTION: ❽

            /* If the standard exception is UNKNOWN */
            if (strcmp (ex_CORBA_UNKNOWN, CORBA_exception_id(&ev) ) == 0 ❾
                {
                /* Retrieve and print the value associated with this failure */
                cur_ex_value = CORBA_exception_value(&ev); ❿
                fprintf(stderr,
                        "Minor error code is:  %d\n",
                        (CORBA_UNKNOWN *)cur_ex_value->minor ⓫
                        );
                fprintf(stderr,
                        "Completion status is: %d\n",
                        (CORBA_UNKNOWN *)cur_ex_value->completed
                        );
                }
            else
                /* If the standard exception is BAD_PARAM */
                if (strcmp (ex_CORBA_BADPARAM , CORBA_exception_id(&ev) ) == 0
                . ⓬
                .
                .
                else
                    {
                    /* unrecognized standard exception */
                    fprintf(stderr,
                            "Internal Error--Unrecognized Standard Exception\n"
                            );
                    }
        break;
```

(continued on next page)

**Example 8–12 (Cont.)  Sample Client Code to Handle Exceptions**

```
/* Internal error check (should never get here) */
default:
     fprintf(stderr,
            "Internal Error in processing exceptions"
            );
break;

};/* end switch */
/* Free storage associated with the exception */
CORBA_exception_free(&ev); ⓭
```

❶ This line shows the declaration of the variable cur_ex_value to be a void *.

❷ This line shows the _major member of the ev structure (which is the environment argument) being used to determine which kind of exception is being signaled and assigning it to its appropriate case for processing.

❸ This line shows that if the value of ev._major is CORBA_NO_EXCEPTION, there is no exception and processing goes to the end of the switch statement.

❹ This line shows that if the value of ev._major is CORBA_USER_EXCEPTION, then processing of the exception takes us through a series of if statements, one for each user-defined exception.

❺ This line shows the identifier for the user-defined exception ex_CORP_HIRING_FREEZE being compared to the identifier for the exception to determine whether this is the ex_CORP_HIRING_FREEZE user-defined exception. The pointer to this identifier is returned by using the CORBA_exception_id routine.

❻ This line shows the variable cur_ex_value being assigned the pointer to the structure associated with the ex_CORP_HIRING_FREEZE user-defined exception. This pointer is returned by using the CORBA_exception_value routine.

❼ This line shows the error code stored in the ex_CORP_HIRING_FREEZE exception being written to the standard error output. Note that the error code is accessed through a pointer to the reason member of the ex_CORP_HIRING_FREEZE user-defined exception structure.

❽ This line shows that if the value of ev._major is CORBA_SYSTEM_EXCEPTION, then processing of the standard exception takes us through a series of if statements, one for each standard exception.

⑨ This line shows the identifier for the standard exception ex_CORBA_UNKNOWN being compared to the identifier for the exception to determine whether this is the ex_CORBA_UNKNOWN standard exception. The pointer to this identifier is returned by using the CORBA_exception_id routine.

⑩ This line shows the variable cur_ex_value being assigned the pointer to the structure associated with the ex_CORBA_UNKNOWN standard exception. This pointer is returned by using the CORBA_exception_value routine.

⑪ This line and the following line show the error information stored in the ex_CORBA_UNKNOWN standard exception being written to the standard error output. Note that the minor error code is accessed through a pointer to the minor member of the ex_CORBA_UNKNOWN standard exception structure, and the completed error code is accessed through a pointer to the completed member of the ex_CORBA_UNKNOWN structure.

⑫ This line shows an ellipsis which represents the if clauses for each of the other standard exceptions. The other standard exceptions are omitted to conserve space.

⑬ This line shows the memory associated with the environment argument ev being freed by using the CORBA_exception_free routine.

# 8.6 Developing a More Complex Client Application

Now that we've discussed developing a simple client application, let's look at some of the other topics that you need to understand when developing a more complex client application:

- Using the context object

- Using dynamic invocation

- Using the interface repository

- Using TypeCodes

## 8.6.1 Using the Context Object

A client application uses the context object to store information about the environment of a request that is not passed as arguments. This information in the context object is stored as a list of properties, each of which consists of the property name and a string value associated with that name.

For example, a context object might contain such information as the end user's preferences for printers, an end user's local symbols, or the server that an end user prefers as a first choice for their requests. Depending on the CORBA vendor, this context object information can then be used by the ORB, server, implementation, or all three, to influence processes such as method binding behavior, server location, or even activation policy.

The context object is defined as part of an operation by using the OMG IDL context clause. A context object is made part of a request by defining it in the interface definition of the operation that is being requested. Any requests for this operation that are invoked by the client will contain the context object as the third argument if C language bindings are used. Example 8–13 shows the context clause on the hire operation on the Personnel interface.

**Example 8–13   Using a Context Object (OMG IDL Code)**

```
/* CORP.IDL */

module CORP
{

/* Define Personnel interface */

interface Personnel : Employee
    {
    Employee hire (in  EmpData      employee_data,
                   in  Department   department_obj,
                   out BadgeNum     new_employee_id)
                   context (display-type, default-printer);
    };// end of interface Personnel
}; //end of module CORP
```

In this example, the context clause specifies that two property names can have values assigned to them, display-type and default-printer. The display-type name is associated with the value of the display device of the end user of the client program, and the default-printer name is associated with the default printer used by the end user of the client program. Because the context clause is part of the hire operation, any request for that operation will have a context object as the third argument if C language bindings are used.

Example 8–14 shows a stub-style invocation of the preceding hire operation on a specific instance of the Personnel object. Note that the context object is required as the third argument, cxt_obj.

**Example 8–14 Using a Context Object (C Code)**

```
/* C */
CORP_Employee CORP_Personnel_hire
    (
    CORP_Personnel    object,
    CORBA_Environment * ev,
    CORBA_Context     cxt_obj,
    CORP_EmpData      * employee_data,
    CORBA_Object      department_obj,
    CORP_BadgeNum     * new_employee_id
    )
```

The following is the procedure a client application uses when it invokes a request for an operation that has the context clause defined (and therefore contains a context object):

1. The client application gets the object reference to the default context object by using the CORBA_ORB_get_default_context operation.

2. The client application can then manage the contents of the default context object in any of the following ways:

   - Retrieve the values of the properties in the context object by using the CORBA_Context_get_values operation.

   - Change the values of the properties in the context object by using the CORBA_Context_set_one_value or CORBA_Context_set_values operation.

   - Add new properties to the context object by using the CORBA_Context_set_one_value operation.

   - Delete properties in the context object by using the CORBA_Context_delete_values operation.

   - Create a child context object, with this context object as the parent, by using the CORBA_Context_create_child operation. Typically, child context objects are created when you want a copy of the context object that is separate, but related to, the parent context object, such as when you want to make a temporary change to a context object.

   Note that CORBA does not require the client application to do anything with the context object, not even to fill in any blank properties. However, your CORBA vendor or framework might have reasons for you to manage the context object in certain ways.

3. The client application invokes the request specifying the object reference to the context object as an argument to the request.

4. When the request is completed, the client might need to perform other tasks on the context object, such as any of the previously listed management tasks.

5. When the client is done using this context object, it then deletes the context object by using the CORBA_Context_delete operation.

Not only can the client application alter the contents of the context object, but the ORB or the implementation can also alter it by adding additional names or values or altering existing values. We'll explain more about how the implementation handles the context object in Chapter 9.

In addition, it is possible that some CORBA vendors might have levels of context objects that can override each other. For example, there could be user, group, and system context objects, with the values in the former overriding the values in the latter; that is, the user overrides the values in the group and the group overrides the values in the system.

Table 8–5 summarizes the context object operations.

**Table 8–5  Summary of Context Object Operations**

| Operation | Description |
| --- | --- |
| CORBA_Context_create_child | Creates a child context object that is chained to its parent context object. Searches on the child context object will also look in the parent context object (and so on up the context object tree) until a match is found. |
| CORBA_Context_delete | Deletes the specified context object. |
| CORBA_Context_delete_values | Deletes the one or more specified property values from the context object. |
| CORBA_Context_get_values | Retrieves the one or more specified property values. |
| CORBA_Context_set_one_value | Adds a single property and value to the context object if the property does not exist. If the property exists, this operation changes the value of the existing property. Currently, only string values are supported by the context object. |
| CORBA_Context_set_values | Sets one or more property values in the context object. Currently, only string values are supported by the context object. |

(continued on next page)

**Table 8-5 (Cont.) Summary of Context Object Operations**

| Operation | Description |
|---|---|
| CORBA_ORB_get_default_context | Gets the object reference to the default context object. |

## 8.6.2 Using Dynamic Invocation

There are two CORBA system components that you use to make dynamic invocation requests:

- Interface repository

- TypeCodes

This section describes considerations in using these components with dynamic invocation.

### 8.6.2.1 Using the Interface Repository

An interface repository is a storage place for modules of interface information, such as the interface information coded in OMG IDL. You can use the interface repository for several purposes in CORBA, such as the following:

- Provide information for the dynamic invocation of a request.

  When you are using dynamic invocation and you know the complete signature of the interface you are requesting, you might not need to use the interface repository. However, most CORBA vendors require the use of the interface repository to validate and probably perform the invocation request.

  If you do not know the signature of the interface operation you are invoking, you can get the one or more OperationDef objects you need for the interface from the interface repository. The OperationDef objects contain the complete signature of the interface operations that you need for dynamic invocation.

- Manage the installation and distribution of interface definitions.

  Using the interface repository lets you manage your interface definitions in a single repository instead of managing multiple individual OMG IDL files. Using the interface repository to store your interface definitions also makes updating those definitions easier because, when you need to update a definition, you need only to update the definition once in the repository instead of updating every OMG IDL file that uses the definition.

Also, if your interface definition includes a number of inherited definitions (such as interfaces, operations, or data type definitions), you can use the interface repository to make sure that the inherited definitions are used when you generate server skeletons or client stubs without having to include the inherited files into the OMG IDL file.

- Provide a mechanism for an interface browser.

  Some CORBA vendors might provide an interface browser that uses the interface repository as its underlying database. This browser might allow interactive browsing and selection of interface definitions from the interfaces available in the repository. Such a browser could be a very useful application development tool.

CORBA defines a set of operations that allow you to access information in the interface repository. How information is placed in the interface repository will vary between CORBA vendors.

Table 8–6 summarizes the operations that CORBA defines to allow access to information in the interface repository. Various CORBA vendors might choose to extend the capabilities of the interface repository beyond the capabilities provided by these operations. Discussing the detailed use of these operations is beyond the scope of this book. These operations are listed here to give you a feeling for the capabilities of the interface repository.

**Table 8–6  Summary of Interface Repository Operations**

| Operation | Description |
| --- | --- |
| CORBA_AttributeDef__get_mode | Returns the mode of access for an attribute. |
| CORBA_AttributeDef__get_type | Returns the TypeCode of an attribute. |
| CORBA_ConstantDef__get_type | Returns the TypeCode for a constant. |
| CORBA_ConstantDef__get_value | Returns the value of a constant. |
| CORBA_Contained_describe | Returns a structure containing all the attributes defined for the contained object. |
| CORBA_Contained__get_defined_in | Returns the RepositoryId for the container where the object is defined. |
| CORBA_Contained__get_id | Returns the RepositoryId of the contained object. |
| CORBA_Contained__get_name | Returns the simple name of the object. |

(continued on next page)

**Table 8–6 (Cont.)  Summary of Interface Repository Operations**

| Operation | Description |
|---|---|
| CORBA_Contained_within | Returns a sequence of objects that contain the object. |
| CORBA_Container_contents | Returns a sequence of objects that are contained by a specified object. |
| CORBA_Container_describe_contents | Returns a description structure for each object contained in a specified object. |
| CORBA_Container_lookup_name | Locates an object by name in a container. |
| CORBA_ExceptionDef__get_type | Returns the data type of an exception definition. |
| CORBA_InterfaceDef_describe_ interface | Provides a full description of all the operations and attributes defined as part of an interface. |
| CORBA_InterfaceDef__get_base_ interfaces | Returns a list of all the interfaces from which the interface inherits. |
| CORBA_OperationDef__get_context | Returns the sequence of context identifiers that apply to an operation definition. |
| CORBA_OperationDef__get_mode | Returns the mode of an operation definition. |
| CORBA_OperationDef__get_result | Returns the TypeCode of the value returned by an operation. |
| CORBA_Repository_lookup_id | Locates an object in the repository when give the object's RepositoryId. |
| CORBA_TypeDef__get_type | Returns the TypeCode for a type definition. |

### 8.6.2.2  Using TypeCodes with Dynamic Invocation

TypeCodes represent invocation argument types and attribute types and
are used to describe basic and user-defined data types. You get a TypeCode
by either retrieving it from an interface repository or by generating it from
an OMG IDL compiler. TypeCodes for new data types that you define can
be generated by an OMG IDL compiler or an interface repository, or both,
depending on your CORBA vendor.

TypeCodes in CORBA have the following uses:

- When using dynamic invocation, TypeCodes can be used to represent
  argument data types.

- In the interface repository, TypeCodes can be used to represent data types
  in certain OMG IDL declarations.

- When using the any data type, TypeCodes can be used to specify which data type is contained in the argument.

CORBA defines TypeCodes to be opaque (like object references); however, CORBA does assume that the C representation of TypeCodes allows TypeCode literals to be placed in C include files.

You manipulate TypeCodes by using the operations defined on the TypeCode object. These operations are not well-defined by CORBA; how they are used will vary among CORBA vendors. Some CORBA vendors might choose to extend these operations to make them more useful. Table 8–7 lists the operations that CORBA defines to manipulate TypeCodes.

**Table 8–7 TypeCode Operations**

| TypeCode Operation | Description |
|---|---|
| CORBA_TypeCode_equal | Used to determine whether two TypeCodes are equivalent. |
| CORBA_TypeCode_kind | Used to determine the data type represented by the TypeCode. |
| CORBA_TypeCode_param_count | Used to determine the number of TypeCode entries in a list. |
| CORBA_TypeCode_parameter | Used to determine the value of the current parameter in a list of TypeCodes. |

A TypeCode represents a kind of field and, if the data type is complex, a parameter list. TypeCodes for simple data types, such as floats and chars, do not have parameter lists. For example, the OMG IDL type long is represented by a TypeCode kind of tk_long with no parameters. On the other hand, a more complex OMG IDL data type, such as sequence<boolean,10>, is represented by a TypeCode kind of tk_sequence with a parameter list containing two parameters, boolean and 10. Two TypeCodes are equal if the OMG IDL type specifications from which they are compiled indicates equal types. If two TypeCodes are equal, they are interchangeable and give identical results when TypeCode operations are applied to them.

Table 8–8 lists the CORBA-defined TypeCodes and their parameters, if they have parameters. Future versions of CORBA will define additional TypeCodes as they are needed.

Table 8–8  CORBA TypeCode Kinds and Parameters

| TypeCode Kind | TypeCode Parameter List |
|---|---|
| tk_any | —[1] |
| tk_array | { TypeCode, length-integer } |
| tk_boolean | —[1] |
| tk_char | —[1] |
| tk_double | —[1] |
| tk_enum | { enum-name, enum-id, ...} |
| tk_float | —[1] |
| tk_long | —[1] |
| tk_null | —[1] |
| tk_objref | { interface-id } |
| tk_octet | —[1] |
| tk_Principal | —[1] |
| tk_sequence | { TypeCode, maximum-length-integer } |
| tk_short | —[1] |
| tk_string | { maximum-length-integer } |
| tk_struct | { struct-name, member-name, TypeCode, ...(repeat pairs) } |
| tk_TypeCode | —[1] |
| tk_ulong | —[1] |
| tk_ushort | —[1] |
| tk_union | { union-name, switch-TypeCode, label-value, member-name, TypeCode, ...(repeat triples) } |
| tk_void | —[1] |

[1]No parameter list is used for this TypeCode.

# 8.7 The Complete Sample Client C Code

Example 8–15 shows the code for our sample client application. The client application accepts the name of an employee as input from an end user and then requests a hire operation on that employee.

**Example 8–15  Complete Sample Client C Code**

```
/* C */

/* Client_main.c  sample personnel client application */

/* Standard C include files */
#include <stdio.h> ❶
#include <stdlib.h>

/* Include typedefs and so on generated from CORP.IDL */
#include "CORP.h" ❷

/* Begin Main client program */

main (int argc, char ** argv)
{
 /* Declarations */ ❸

  CORBA_Object         pers_obj;       /* Personnel object */
  CORBA_Object         dep_obj;        /* Department object */
  CORBA_Object         emp_obj;        /* Employee object */
  CORBA_Status         status;
  CORBA_Environment     ev;
  FILE                 * temp_file;
  CORBA_char           string_obj [1024];
  CORP_EmpData         emp_data;
  CORP_BadgeNum        badge_num;

  /*....................................................................*/

  /* Get employee information from the end user*/ ❶
  if (argc < 7)
      {
      fprintf(stderr,
              "Usage : %s department last first middle class rate\n",
              argv[0]);
      exit(0);
      }
```

(continued on next page)

**Example 8–15 (Cont.)   Complete Sample Client C Code**

```c
/* Get the personnel object from the file */
temp_file = fopen("PersFile.dat", "r"); ❺
if (temp_file == NULL)
    {
    fprintf(stderr,
            "Could not open file to get Personnel object reference\n",
            argv[1]);
    exit(0);
    }
if (fgets(string_obj, sizeof(string_obj), temp_file) == NULL)
    {
    fprintf(stderr,
            "Could not read the Personnel object from the file\n");
    exit(0);
    }
fclose(temp_file);

/* Convert the string-formatted Personnel object reference to a binary-formatted
   object reference */

pers_obj = CORBA_ORB_string_to_object ( ❻
                                CORBA_Vendor_ORB_OBJECT, ❼
                                & ev,
                                string_obj);

if (ev . _major != CORBA_NO_EXCEPTION || pers_obj == (CORBA_Object) NULL) ❽
    {
    CORBA_exception_free( & ev );
    CORBA_Object_release(pers_obj, & ev);
    Vendor_ORB_rundown( CORBA_Vendor_ORB_OBJECT,       ❾
                        (CORBA_Environment *)NULL,
                        (CORBA_Flags)0 );
    exit(0);
    }

/* Get the Department object from the file using the Department name passed in */
temp_file = fopen(argv[1], "r"); ❿
if (temp_file == NULL)
    {
    fprintf(stderr,
            "Could not open File %s to get Department object reference\n",
            argv[1]);
    exit(0);
    }
```

(continued on next page)

**Example 8–15 (Cont.)  Complete Sample Client C Code**

```
if (fgets(string_obj, sizeof(string_obj), temp_file) == NULL)
    {
    fprintf(stderr,
            "Could not read the Department object reference from the file\n");
    exit(0);
    }
fclose(temp_file);

/* Convert the string-formatted Department object reference to a binary-formatted
   object reference */

dep_obj = CORBA_ORB_string_to_object (
                                 CORBA_Vendor_ORB_OBJECT,
                                 & ev,
                                 string_obj);

if (ev . _major != CORBA_NO_EXCEPTION || dep_obj == (CORBA_Object) NULL)
    {
    CORBA_exception_free( & ev );
    CORBA_Object_release(dep_obj, & ev);
    Vendor_ORB_rundown( CORBA_Vendor_ORB_OBJECT,
                        (CORBA_Environment *)NULL,
                        (CORBA_Flags)0 );
    exit(0);
    }

/* Fill out the emp_data argument */ ⓫
emp_data . last_name = argv[2];
emp_data . first_name = argv[3];
emp_data . middle_name = argv[4];
emp_data . job_class = * argv[5];
emp_data . hourly_rate = atof(argv[6]);

/* Hire the employee */
emp_obj = CORP_Personnel_hire(pers_obj, &ev, &emp_data, dep_obj, & badge_num); ⓬
if (ev . _major != CORBA_NO_EXCEPTION)
    {
    printf("Could not hire the employee\n");
    CORBA_exception_free( & ev );
    CORBA_Object_release(dep_obj, & ev);
    CORBA_Object_release(pers_obj, & ev);
    Vendor_ORB_rundown( CORBA_Vendor_ORB_OBJECT,
                        (CORBA_Environment *)NULL,
                        (CORBA_Flags)0 );
    exit( 0 );
    }
```

(continued on next page)

**Example 8–15 (Cont.) Complete Sample Client C Code**

```
/* Get the employee's data to verify the data is correct */
emp_data = CORP_Employee_get_EmpData(emp_obj, &ev);  ⑬
if (ev . _major != CORBA_NO_EXCEPTION)
    {
    fprintf(stderr,"Could not get the employee data \n");
    CORBA_exception_free( & ev );
    CORBA_Object_release(emp_obj, & ev);
    CORBA_Object_release(dep_obj, & ev);
    CORBA_Object_release(pers_obj, & ev);
    Vendor_ORB_rundown( CORBA_Vendor_ORB_OBJECT,
                        (CORBA_Environment *)NULL,
                        (CORBA_Flags)0 );

    exit(0);
    }
/* Echo employee data back to the end user */        ⑭
printf("Hiring process complete for employee:\n");
printf("\tLast Name : \t%s\n", emp_data . last_name);
printf("\tFirst Name : \t%s\n", emp_data . first_name);
printf("\tMiddle Name : \t%s\n", emp_data . middle_name);
printf("\tJob Class : \t%c\n", emp_data . job_class);
printf("\tHourly Rate: %f\n", emp_data . hourly_rate);

/* Release all memory associated with emp_data argument */  ⑮
CORBA_free(emp_data . last_name);
CORBA_free(emp_data . first_name);
CORBA_free(emp_data . middle_name);

/* Release all of the objects */  ⑯
CORBA_Object_release(emp_obj, & ev);
CORBA_Object_release(dep_obj, & ev);
CORBA_Object_release(pers_obj, & ev);
if (ev . _major != CORBA_NO_EXCEPTION)
exit(0);

} /* end of main */
```

❶ This line and the following lines show the inclusion of the C libraries required by this program.

❷ This line shows the inclusion of the file CORP.h that contains typedefs and other header information generated from CORP.IDL.

❸ This line and the following lines show the declarations used for this program.

❹ This line and the following lines show the program getting information on the employee to be hired from the end user of the client application.

⑤ This line and the following lines show the client application getting the object reference for the personnel object from a file.

⑥ This line shows the string form of the personnel object reference being changed to an actual object reference by using the CORBA_ORB_string_to_obj operation.

⑦ This line shows that the first argument to the CORBA_ORB_string_to_object routine is an object reference to the ORB itself, in this example, CORBA_Vendor_ORB_OBJECT. Each CORBA vendor has a different ORB; in this example, the name CORBA_Vendor_ORB_OBJECT indicates a particular vendor's ORB.

⑧ This line and the following lines show simple error checking and memory management on the retrieval of the personnel object. If there is an exception signaled, or if the personnel object is NULL, then the personnel object has not been successfully retrieved. Because the application did not get the personnel object, it needs to free the memory associated with the environment argument and the personnel object, and then do any necessary ORB-related cleanup.

⑨ This line shows the CORBA vendor-specific operation Vendor_ORB_rundown. A vendor might provide something like this operation to handle various clean-up tasks for the vendor's ORB, such as the release of resources no longer used, network resources, and ORB-internal memory deallocation that the application cannot handle itself.

⑩ This line and the following lines show the client application getting the object reference for the department object from the file and then having it converted from a string to an object reference by using the CORBA_ORB_string_to_obj operation.

This coding is very similar to the previous code that handled getting the personnel object reference.

⑪ This line and the following lines show the emp_data structure getting filled with data. This argument will be used in the request for the hire operation.

⑫ This line and the following lines show the invocation of the request for the employee to be hired. The CORP_Personnel_hire operation an object reference for the new employee and requires the following arguments that have previously been retrieved:

The personnel object reference, pers_obj
The always present environment argument, ev
The employee data, emp_data

The department object, dep_obj
The badge number created, badge_num

**⑬** This line and the following lines show the application performing an invocation of a request to get the new employee's data to make sure it was created correctly.

**⑭** This line and the following lines show the application telling the end user that the employee has been successfully hired.

**⑮** This line and the following lines show the application releasing the memory associated with the emp_data structure, now that the employee has been successfully hired.

**⑯** This line and the following lines show the application releasing the memory associated with the object references for the personnel, department, and employee objects, now that the employee has been successfully hired.

# 9

# Developing the Server Side of the Application

Now that we've discussed how to write a client that invokes requests, we are ready to discuss how to write the server where the requested operation is actually performed. Servers contain implementations that can respond to requests from clients. An implementation does the requested work using methods within the implementation.

Throughout this chapter, we assume that the BOA is the object adapter being used by the server application, because CORBA does not currently specify any other object adapter. We'll discuss how to develop the server side of a CORBA application by first discussing what the BOA does and the operations defined on the BOA. We'll then look at how an object is created, does its work, and is destroyed, and how the BOA fits into this process. Finally, we'll discuss the steps involved in actually building a server application.

## 9.1 Using the BOA

An object adapter is the primary mechanism for managing object references and implementations on the server. The BOA is the object adapter that all CORBA vendors must supply as part of their systems. In CORBA, the BOA is designed to be the most commonly used object adapter.

Some CORBA vendors might provide additional specialized object adapters, such as library object adapters or object-oriented database adapters; however, those object adapters and how they function will likely be vendor specific. In this section, we will focus on the BOA because it is the only object adapter defined by CORBA, and it is likely that the more specialized vendor-specific object adapters will be very similar to it.

The BOA, together with the server skeletons generated from the interface definitions, contains the information needed to map a client's request for an operation on an object from the ORB to the appropriate implementation and method on the server.

The BOA causes an implementation to be activated and can also cause it to be deactivated, depending on how your CORBA vendor handles implementation deactivation. In addition, the BOA provides a group of operations that allow the server application developer to manage objects, object references, and implementations on the server. Table 9–1 lists the operations defined as part of the BOA. Some CORBA vendors might have additional operations defined on their BOA to support certain features of their CORBA system.

**Table 9–1  Operations Defined as Part of the BOA**

| Operation | Capability Provided |
|---|---|
| CORBA_BOA_change_implementation | Switches the implementation used. |
| CORBA_BOA_create | Creates an object reference. |
| CORBA_BOA_deactivate_impl | Notifies the BOA that an implementation is deactivated if that implementation is associated with the shared server or persistent server activation policies. |
| CORBA_BOA_deactivate_obj | Notifies the BOA that an implementation is deactivated if that implementation is associated with the unshared server **activation policy**. |
| CORBA_BOA_dispose | Destroys an object reference. |
| CORBA_BOA_get_id | Retrieves information about an object reference that typically uniquely identifies that object reference. |
| CORBA_BOA_get_principal | Retrieves authentication information. |
| CORBA_BOA_impl_is_ready | Notifies the BOA that an implementation is activated and ready to receive client requests if that implementation is associated with the shared server or persistent server activation policies. |
| CORBA_BOA_obj_is_ready | Notifies the BOA that an implementation is activated and ready to receive client requests if that implementation is associated with the unshared server activation policy. |
| CORBA_BOA_set_exception | Sets an exception to raise an error condition. |

Although CORBA spells out the operations and capabilities that the BOA must provide, it does not describe how many of these should be accomplished. How the BOA is associated with the ORB, the server, or (through the server skeletons) the methods in the implementations on the server will vary between CORBA vendors. For example, the BOA can be associated with these parts of the system through some look-up mechanism, such as a name service or a registry, or through some other means.

## 9.2 The Life Cycle of a CORBA Object

All real-life objects, such as employees, are represented as object references in a CORBA system. A CORBA client typically uses references to objects to make requests for operations to be performed. The server, on the other hand, actually performs most of the manipulation of the objects themselves through the methods in its implementations.

These manipulations of objects follow a pattern called a **life cycle**. The life cycle of an object is the same as the life cycle of any other entity: a life cycle is the progress of an object through various stages in its life, from creation to destruction. It is important to understand the life cycle of an object because it lets you better understand how objects are used in an object-oriented system like CORBA.

Figure 9–1 illustrates the life cycle of an object in CORBA when using the BOA as the object adapter.

**Figure 9–1  Life Cycle of a CORBA Object**

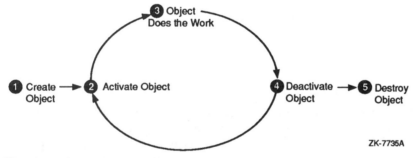

ZK-7735A

❶ Create object

A reference to an object is created by using the CORBA_BOA_create operation. When an object reference is created, the real-world object is identified to the CORBA system and is associated with both an interface and an implementation. Chapter 10 describes how an implementation is associated with an interface.

For example, if an employee were hired by a company, an object reference would be created for that employee so the employee could be represented in the company's computer systems. The interface to employee objects would describe the operations that could be performed on an instance of an employee object, and the implementation of the employee object would actually perform the operations that could be requested on the employee.

❷ Activate object

For an object's implementation to be used in a CORBA system, it needs to be activated so that it can be used to satisfy client requests. When the BOA receives a client request, it finds an implementation that can satisfy that request and activates it. When the implementation is completely activated, the implementation notifies the BOA that it is ready to receive client requests by using either the CORBA_BOA_impl_is_ready or the CORBA_BOA_obj_is_ready operation, depending on the activation policy associated with the implementation. We'll discuss activation policies in detail in Section 9.4.1.

❸ Object does the work

Once the BOA has been notified that the implementation is activated and ready to receive requests, the implementation can receive client requests from the BOA and perform those requests by using the methods contained within the implementation.

For example, once an implementation of the employee object has been activated and the BOA has been notified of this, the server in which the implementation is activated can satisfy client requests for operations on an employee object by using the implementation of the employee object.

❹ Deactivate object

At some point, an implementation is no longer available to satisfy client requests and needs to be deactivated. An implementation notifies the BOA that it will no longer accept client requests and is going to be deactivated by using either the CORBA_BOA_deactivate_impl or CORBA_BOA_deactivate_obj operation, depending on the activation policy associated with the implementation. After the implementation has notified the BOA, the implementation is deactivated either by the BOA or through some other mechanism.

An example of when you might want to deactivate an object would be when the object is not in use and has no outstanding object references.

❺ Destroy object

At some point, an object reference is destroyed by using the CORBA_BOA_dispose operation. An object reference should be destroyed when the real-world object it describes is no longer used by the system. When an object reference is destroyed, it is as if it never existed in the system, and any requests for operations on that particular object reference will fail because it does not exist.

For example, if an employee were dismissed from a company, the object reference associated with that employee would be destroyed, because the employee would no longer be part of the company or its systems.

Now that you know the life cycle of an object in CORBA, and how the BOA figures into that life cycle, let's discuss how one actually goes about building a CORBA server.

# 9.3 General Process of Building a CORBA Server

In this section, we will describe the general process of building a CORBA server. A CORBA server can take different forms: a server could be a process, an instance of a dynamically loaded library, or something else. Your CORBA vendor will probably describe what they consider to be valid servers for their software. Here and in the following sections, we will assume that the object adapter being used is the BOA because it is the only object adapter that must be present in every vendor's CORBA system.

When you develop a server application, you will perform the following general steps:

1. Determine the activation policy the implementation will support.

   Specify the activation policy information about your server to the BOA in whatever way your CORBA vendor provides. We'll discuss activation policies in detail in Section 9.4.1.

2. Generate the server skeletons.

   You generate the server skeletons from the interface definitions for the interfaces that you'll support with implementations. Server skeletons indicate which kinds of objects can be referenced and which implementations are available for activation by the BOA.

3. Connect those skeletons to your server application and to the object adapter, which is usually the BOA.

   The object adapter handles general ORB-related tasks such as providing object references, activating implementations, and so on.

The server skeleton takes these general tasks and ties them to particular implementations and their contained methods in the server.

Typically, you connect the skeletons to the server application by compiling and linking the skeleton code to the server application code. This is similar to the way you connect the client stub to a client application.

4. Write the code to initialize the server.

   The routines you use to initialize the server will vary from vendor to vendor. But in general, you will need to do the initialization needed to start any server process, and then do the initialization needed for the server to be made known to the CORBA system.

5. Write the code to notify the BOA that the implementation has been activated.

   As we mentioned when we described the life cycle of an object, once an implementation is created in the CORBA system, it needs to be activated so that it can be used to satisfy client requests. The BOA causes the implementation to be activated as a result of receiving an appropriate client request.

   When the implementation has completed activation, the implementation notifies the BOA that it is ready to receive client requests by using either the CORBA_BOA_impl_is_ready or CORBA_BOA_obj_is_ready operation, depending on the activation policy associated with the implementation.

   Between the time that the server is started and the time that the BOA is notified that the implementation is activated, the BOA prevents any requests from being delivered to that implementation in that server.

6. Write the code to create a dispatching loop.

   How you write your server is influenced by the capabilities your CORBA vendor gives you and the assumptions the vendor makes about how your server will work. Most CORBA vendors assume that CORBA servers will be designed to be event driven; that is, the servers will be written to respond to events in the CORBA system, such as client requests. In most cases, you will need to write some kind of dispatching loop so that your server can accept and respond to these events; this loop will probably be the main portion of your server program.

   If your CORBA system does not assume that the server will be event driven, then you will use some other mechanism to route client requests to the appropriate methods that will perform the requested tasks.

7. Write the methods to support the implementations listed in your skeletons.

   This is the code that does the actual work of the implementation, including handling context objects, raising exceptions, creating and destroying object references, and so on.

   You might want to write some general convenience routines as part of your implementation or server to be used by your methods, if your methods tend to perform certain common functions, such as routines to do memory or object management.

8. Write the code to deactivate the implementation.

   At some point, an implementation needs to be deactivated so that it is no longer available to satisfy client requests from the BOA. For example, an implementation might need to be deactivated before the server is shut down or when it has been unused for too long a period of time.

   You use either the CORBA_BOA_deactivate_impl operation or the CORBA_BOA_deactivate_obj operation to notify the BOA that an implementation is going to be deactivated. The operation you use depends on the activation policy associated with the implementation. Once the BOA has been notified, you can then actually deactivate the implementation by using a vendor-specific BOA operation or whatever other mechanism your CORBA vendor has provided.

9. Write the code to shut down the server.

   As with the code needed to initialize the server, the routines you use to shut down the server will probably be vendor specific. The shutdown procedure that you write will also need to do the CORBA-specific shutdown of the server first and then do the actual shutdown of the server process if necessary.

10. If this application also can be a client as well as a server, also follow the process to build a client described in Chapter 8.

We'll discuss these steps in more detail in the following sections. Figure 9–2 illustrates and summarizes the code that a server logically contains.

# .4  Writing a Server

In this section, we will discuss how to develop the parts of a server application, from determining the activation policy to associate with an implementation to how you use various operations to perform tasks in your methods.

We cannot show you a complete server because the details of how you write
your server varies greatly between CORBA vendors. We can only show you a
series of comments in a C source file that would indicate the general structure
of a server as illustrated in Figure 9–2.

**Figure 9–2  Logical Structure of a Server**

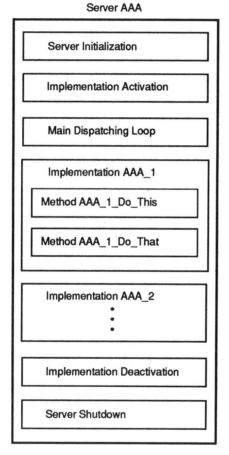

ZK-7736A

# 9.4.1 Deciding on an Activation Policy for the Implementation

When an object reference is created, it is bound to an interface and to an implementation. You use an activation policy to control whether the BOA can activate the implementation. For example, if an implementation has the persistent server activation policy, the BOA cannot start it because the activation policy defines that the implementation is always available. The BOA supports several activation policies because CORBA recognizes that the BOA cannot satisfy all implementations with a single activation policy.

Your CORBA vendor will determine how an activation policy is associated with an implementation. Most vendors will place this information in the server skeletons through some mechanism, such as looking up the information in the implementation repository, or by reading some intermediate files that are used with the interface definitions to generate the server skeletons.

You define activation policies on object implementations. A process that contains an object implementation might contain more than one object implementation, thus there could be more than one activation policy.

The following sections describe the activation policies that the BOA must support. The policies are ordered from the most used to the least commonly used. Some CORBA vendors might extend these activation policies for some reason, either by adding additional activation policies for their BOA or by adding other mechanisms to qualify the CORBA-defined activation policies.

## 9.4.1.1 Shared Server Activation Policy

The most commonly used activation policy for an implementation is the shared server activation policy. An implementation with a shared server activation policy can manage multiple active instances of the objects supported by the implementation at the same time. When you use the shared server activation policy, you need to make sure your server can handle the possibility of one or more objects being accessed at the same time. A good use for the shared server activation policy would be for an implementation that typically handles several related objects simultaneously.

An implementation with the shared server activation policy performs its work in the following manner:

1. The BOA starts the server in which this implementation resides.

2. The server and implementation initialize themselves.

3. The BOA activates the implementation in response to an appropriate client request. When the implementation is completely activated, the implementation uses the CORBA_BOA_impl_is_ready operation to notify the BOA that it is ready to receive client requests.

4. The implementation does its work with potentially several objects active at the same time.

5. When finished, the implementation uses the CORBA_BOA_deactivate_impl operation to notify the BOA that it can no longer receive client requests.

### 9.4.1.2  Persistent Server Activation Policy

An implementation with a persistent server activation policy is really just a special case of the shared server activation policy. The difference is in how a server supporting the implementation is started.

With the shared server activation policy, the BOA starts a server that supports an implementation. Whereas, with the persistent server activation policy, there is some way other than the BOA to start a server. Startup is probably outside of CORBA altogether, such as in a system startup file.

Once started, a server that supports an implementation with the persistent server activation policy behaves just as if it supported the shared server activation policy, including having all the attributes of the shared server activation policy, such as the ability to support multiple active objects.

A good use for the persistent server activation policy would be when only one version of the server can be running for some reason, or when a specific setup for that server is required, or when the application using that server counts on that implementation always being available, without needing to start it.

An implementation with the persistent server activation policy performs its work in the same manner as an implementation with the shared server activation policy, except that the server is started by means other than the BOA.

### 9.4.1.3  Unshared Server Activation Policy

An implementation with an unshared server activation policy handles only a single object at a time and is dedicated to handling that particular object. In a real sense, the implementation becomes that object rather than being a manager of multiple objects of the same type like an implementation with the shared or persistent server activation policies.

You might find it useful to think of the unshared server activation policy as "server per object" because it requires a separate dedicated server for each object associated with an implementation that has this activation type. As a result of being dedicated to a single object, the associated implementation and server have exclusive control over this particular object. Multiple clients can share the same server, as long as those clients are all making requests of the same particular implementation and object.

A good use for the unshared server activation policy would be for an implementation that handles only a single specific object. Examples of such specific objects that need a dedicated implementation would be objects used to encapsulate existing legacy applications or to encapsulate scarce resources, such as a specialized plotter.

An implementation with the unshared server activation policy performs its work in the following manner:

1. The BOA starts the server in which the implementation resides.

2. The server and implementation initialize themselves.

3. The BOA activates the implementation in response to an appropriate client request. When it is completely activated, the implementation uses the CORBA_BOA_obj_is_ready operation to notify the BOA that it is ready to receive client requests.

4. The implementation does its work with potentially several clients simultaneously using the same active object. If a client request is for an object that is not yet active, the BOA will start a new server for that object and implementation.

5. The implementation uses the CORBA_BOA_deactivate_obj operation to notify the BOA that it will no longer receive client requests and then the implementation is deactivated using a CORBA vendor-specific BOA operation or some other means.

## 9.4.1.4 Server Per Method Activation Policy

The server per method activation policy is the least commonly used activation policy for an implementation. Each time an implementation with this activation policy invokes a method, a new instance of a server is created for that method to execute in; when that method is completed, that instance of a server is terminated. What constitutes an instance of a server can vary between CORBA systems.

Several implementations for the same object, or even the same method, can be active simultaneously, one for each outstanding request. Because a new server is started for each request, it is not necessary for the implementation to notify the BOA when the implementation is being activated or deactivated. The BOA activates an implementation for each request, regardless of whether another request for that operation, object, or implementation is active at the same time.

A good use for the server per method activation policy would be for implementations that use scripts; for example, when a script is used to encapsulate a legacy application. Another good use for these implementations is for "one-shot" implementations, such as an implementation that performs a compile or executes a startup file, and then exits when done.

An implementation with the server per method activation policy performs its work in the following manner:

1. The BOA starts the server on which the implementation resides.

2. The server and implementation initialize themselves.

3. The implementation does its work. Each time an implementation invokes a method, a new server is created for that method to execute in; when the method is completed, that server is terminated. What constitutes a new server can vary by CORBA vendor: a new server could be a new process, a new instance of a dynamically loaded library, or something else.

   As we discussed earlier, because a new server is started for each request, it is not necessary for the implementation to notify the BOA when the implementation is being activated or deactivated.

## 9.4.2 Generating and Linking in Server Skeletons

A server skeleton is similar to a client stub in that it connects information from the interface definitions to an application. The client stub connects this information to a client application that is using stub-style invocation and a server skeleton connects this information to a server application.

A server skeleton makes it possible for the ORB and an object adapter to translate your client request to a specific method in an implementation in a server. The server skeleton contains programming language-specific code that maps client requests for operations into procedural routines that the skeleton will call when a corresponding request arrives; typically, the procedural routines map to the methods in the implementation.

Once you have determined how your implementation will be activated, you can then generate the server skeletons for the implementations you will support and link them into your server. We discussed how to select an activation policy before generating the server skeletons because some CORBA vendors place the activation policy information in the server skeletons when you generate them.

You generate your server skeletons from the interface definitions that your server will support with implementations. These server skeletons indicate which kinds of objects can be referenced or supported and which implementations are available for activation by the BOA. How you generate the server skeletons will vary depending on your CORBA vendor, but you will probably generate them from either an OMG IDL compiler that uses your interface definitions as input or from an implementation repository that has loaded your interface definitions.

Once the server skeletons are generated, you need to connect them to your server code in some way. CORBA does not specify how to connect the server skeleton to the server application, but typically most CORBA vendors connect them by generating the server skeletons in source code format and then having you compile and then link the server skeleton and the server object code together. This is similar to the manner you connected the client stubs to your client application.

You will also need to associate your server skeletons with an appropriate object adapter, such as the BOA. You use whatever mechanism your CORBA vendor provides to associate your server skeletons with an object adapter. The object adapter handles general ORB-related tasks such as providing object references, activating implementations, and so on. The server skeleton takes these general tasks and ties them to particular implementations and their contained methods in the server. In this section, we are assuming the BOA as the object adapter, because that is the object adapter supplied by all CORBA vendors.

Example 9–1 shows an example of server skeletons being generated, compiled, and then linked into a server program on a UNIX system. The exact syntax and commands used will vary with your programming language, operating system, and CORBA vendor. Example 9–1 is annotated and keyed to the following list of explanations.

**Example 9–1  Generating and Connecting Server Skeletons**

```
/* OMG IDL */
> ls ❶
CORP.idl        server_main.c   server_main.o
>

> idl_compile -s CORP_sskel.c CORP.idl ❷
> ls
CORP.idl        CORP.h          CORP_sskel.c
server_main.c   server_main.o
>

>cc CORP_sskel.c ❸
>ls
CORP.idl        CORP.h          CORP_sskel.c
CORP_sskel.o    server_main.c   server_main.o
>
```

(continued on next page)

**Example 9–1 (Cont.)  Generating and Connecting Server Skeletons**

```
>cc -o server_main CORP_main.o CORP_sskels.o -l ORB ❶
>ls
CORP.idl        CORP.h          CORP_cstub.c
CORP_cstub.o    server_main     server_main.c
server_main.o
>
```

❶  The ls command is a UNIX command for listing the contents of a directory.
   The following code displays the files in the directory:

   CORP.idl, displays the OMG IDL source file
   server_main.c, displays the main server application source file
   server_main.o, displays the main server application object file

❷  This line shows the idl_compile command being used to activate the
   example OMG IDL compiler.  Here, the OMG IDL source file, CORP.idl, is
   specified as input and the -s CORP_sskel.c option indicates that a server
   skeleton with that name should be created.

   As a result, this compiler generates the server skeleton file CORP_sskel.c
   and also a C header file for the CORP module, CORP.h.

❸  This line shows the server skeleton CORP_sskel.c, being compiled by the C
   compiler, resulting in the object file CORP_sskel.o.

❹  This line shows the executable file, server_main, being created by linking
   together the server skeleton object file CORP_sskel.o, the main server
   application object file server_main.o, and the CORBA vendor's ORB
   library ORB where the CORBA routines are defined.

## 9.4.3  Writing the Code to Start and Stop a Server

In CORBA, object adapters such as the BOA start and stop servers by using
operating system-specific mechanisms, such as starting and stopping processes.
Starting up and shutting down a server are two closely related tasks, because
what you need to do to start a server needs to be undone to stop it.  Because
these tasks are closely related, we'll talk about them together in this section.

The server code you need to write to start and initialize or shut down and stop
your server will vary, depending on your programming language, operating
system, and CORBA vendor.  However, you will need to write code that does
the following tasks no matter what language, computer, or CORBA vendor
combination you have chosen.

### 9.4.3.1 Starting and Initializing a CORBA Server

To start and initialize a CORBA server you need to perform the following
procedure:

1. Write code that performs general non-CORBA server initialization tasks,
   such as setting data into any data structures the server needs to do its
   work.

2. Write code that performs general CORBA-specific server initialization
   tasks, such as creating any initial object references the server needs to
   make available to itself or to client applications.

3. Write code that tells the object adapter (the BOA) how to start your server.
   Because it is the BOA that actually starts and stops your server, you need
   to tell the BOA how to do that. How you give this information to the BOA
   will vary, depending on your CORBA vendor; you can pass this information
   to the BOA by using a data file, a set of definitions, or through some other
   procedure.

   Whatever the procedure, this information will need to contain at least the
   command string used to actually start the server running on the operating
   system, such as /ORB/servers/server1 -c, if implemented as an operating
   system process. In addition, the activation policy associated with the
   implementations on the server is likely specified here as well, although
   some vendors might start the implementations and then query them to
   determine what activation policy each supports.

4. Write code that tells the BOA that an active instance of a server exists and
   can be used. This code identifies to the BOA the skeletons that can be used
   to access the implementation. Again, how you pass this information to the
   BOA will be specific to your selected CORBA vendor, but will likely be done
   through some set of vendor-specific routines.

   If your CORBA system supports only a single implementation for each
   server, you may not need to perform this task, because anytime that server
   is active it will be for the same implementation.

### 9.4.3.2 Stopping a CORBA Server

Stopping a CORBA server, as with most servers, is primarily a matter of
undoing everything you did in starting the server. To shut down and stop a
CORBA server, you need to perform the following tasks in the following order:

1. Write code that tells the BOA that an active instance of a server no longer
   exists and therefore cannot be used. How you pass this information to the
   BOA will be specific to your selected CORBA vendor, but will likely be done
   through some set of vendor-specific routines.

Some CORBA vendors will take care of this task for you as part of the deactivation process. If your CORBA system supports only a single implementation for each server, you also may not need to perform this task, because anytime that server is not active, the associated implementation will not be active.

2. Tell the object adapter (the BOA) how to stop your server. Because it is the BOA that actually stops your server, you need tell the BOA how to do that. How you give this information to the BOA will vary depending on your CORBA vendor: you can pass this information to the BOA using a data file, a set of definitions, or some other procedure. The BOA will likely stop your server in some manner that is specific to the operating system on which the server is running, such as stopping a process or unloading a dynamically loaded library.

3. Write code that performs general CORBA-specific server shutdown tasks, such as destroying any object references used by the server itself.

4. Write code that performs general non-CORBA server shutdown tasks, such as closing any files and freeing the memory associated with any data structures the server used to do its work.

### 9.4.4 Writing the Code to Activate and Deactivate Your Implementations

As with starting and stopping a server, activating and deactivating implementations on a server are two closely related tasks, and therefore we'll discuss them together in this section.

When the BOA receives a client request, it finds an implementation that can perform that requested operation with an appropriate activation policy and activates that implementation unless it is already activated. Until the implementation is activated, no request can be sent to it. When the implementation is completely activated, the implementation notifies the BOA that it is ready to receive client requests.

Similarly, when it is time to deactivate an implementation, such as when the server is going to be shut down, the implementation notifies the BOA that it can no longer receive client requests. How you notify the BOA that an implementation is activated or will be deactivated depends on the activation policy associated with the implementation. Table 9–2 summarizes the operations you use to notify the BOA that an implementation is activated or will be deactivated, depending on which activation policy is associated with the implementation.

**Table 9–2  Operations Used to Notify the BOA About Implementation Activation and Deactivation**

| Implementation Activation Policy | Operation to Notify BOA | |
| --- | --- | --- |
| | Implementation Activation | Implementation Deactivation |
| Shared Server | CORBA_BOA_impl_is_ready | CORBA_BOA_deactivate_impl |
| Persistent Server | CORBA_BOA_impl_is_ready | CORBA_BOA_deactivate_impl |
| Unshared Server | CORBA_BOA_obj_is_ready | CORBA_BOA_deactivate_obj |
| Server Per Method | None[1] | None[1] |

[1]When an implementation has the server per method activation policy, the implementation does not need to notify the BOA when the implementation is to be activated or deactivated, and therefore these operations are not used.

How implementation activation and deactivation actually occurs, and how much code you will need to write to make it happen will vary by CORBA vendor. However implementation activation and deactivation is handled, you will probably want to handle more than just that in your server.

When you activate an implementation, you will probably do more than just issue the appropriate operation. You will probably also include code to do any initialization that is required by the implementation that was not taken care of by the server, such as creating any initial objects or files that the implementation needs to do its job.

Similarly, when you deactivate an implementation, you will want to do whatever implementation shutdown is needed as well as notifying the BOA using the appropriate operation. As part of this shutdown, you can do such things as destroying any associated objects, closing any files, or freeing any memory that the implementation used to do its job.

Another thing to keep in mind in writing your activation and deactivation code is that activating or deactivating an implementation is not necessarily done only once in a server; you can regularly activate and deactivate implementations in order to minimize the number of implementations available in the system or for other reasons.

## 9.4.5 Dispatching Client Requests to the Implementation Methods

How you write your server is influenced by the capabilities your CORBA vendor gives you and the assumptions the vendor makes about how your server will work. Most vendors assume that CORBA servers will be designed to be event driven; that is, the servers will be written to respond to events in the system. Typically, these events will be client requests from the BOA that need to be sent along to the appropriate implementation and method.

Typically, developers write dispatching loops to handle events. Dispatching loops are fairly common in programming and are used to handle events, such as X Window System events, PC window events, or some other events. This dispatching loop is where your server can spend a good deal of its time waiting for incoming requests, and will probably be in the main portion of your program.

The way that a dispatching loop works is that the server waits in the dispatching loop until it receives an event of some kind. Typically, a CORBA event would be the result of a client request, but it could also be the result of some other activity in the ORB or the BOA, such as notification that some transport socket has been disconnected.

When the server receives the event for a client request, the server verifies that the server contains an implementation that can respond to the request. Then the server skeleton directs the request to the appropriate method in the implementation and the methods do whatever is necessary to satisfy the requested operation. When the event is for some internal activity, the ORB or BOA handles the event the way the vendor finds most appropriate. If your CORBA vendor allows you to develop custom event-handling mechanisms, it is best not to assume that every event will be for a client request, unless your CORBA vendor assures you that that is the case.

How you write this dispatching loop and what routines you use will depend on your CORBA vendor and your own needs, such as whether you need to integrate your CORBA events with other types of events into a single dispatching scheme.

CORBA does not require you to have a dispatcher that handles only one type of event as some distributed systems do; in fact, your vendor's CORBA events might be able to be integrated with other events into a single dispatcher relatively easily. Having a single dispatcher for all your events is much easier to code and maintain than is having several dispatchers, each handling their own types of events. Being able to have a single dispatcher also lets you more easily encapsulate legacy applications that have their own events that need to be dispatched.

Some CORBA vendors will assume you want to do such integration and provide you with mechanisms to support it, other vendors might supply you with a dispatching loop dedicated to their CORBA events and a set of routines to use within it, and other CORBA vendors might leave it to entirely to you to decide how to set up the loop.

## 9.4.6 Writing Methods

Methods are the pieces of code in an implementation that actually do the work that satisfies a client request. The server matches each operation that a client requests to a method in the associated implementation.

CORBA does not restrict the form of methods. You can write methods in any form you find useful that your CORBA vendor and your programming language supports, such as routines, scripts, entry points into shareable libraries, or any other supported form.

For the C language, CORBA specifies that when you are using the BOA as the object adapter, the signature of a method supporting an operation must be the same as the signature defined for a client stub used to invoke that operation. You specify object references, environments, context objects, and other arguments. What is new in the method code is that you can use BOA operations to perform some of the tasks your method needs to accomplish—we'll talk about those operations in the following sections.

For other vendor-specific object adapters, the signature of the method is not guaranteed to be the same as the related client stub. For example, other object adapters can provide additional arguments to the method to allow access to features in that object adapter.

Example 9–2 shows a method for the `hire` operation to be performed on a `NewEmployee` object.

**Example 9–2  Formatting a Method**

```
/* C */
void CORP_NewEmployee_hire
(
CORP_New_Employee  object,      ❶
CORBA_Environment  *ev,         ❷
CORBA_Context      cxt_obj,     ❸
CORBA_char         job_class    ❹
)
```

❶ This line indicates the `object` argument. This argument is the object reference to the specific new employee object that is to have the `hire` operation performed on it.

❷ This line indicates the environment argument that can contain exception information from the request.

❸ This line indicates the `cxt_obj` argument. This argument is the object reference to the specific context object associated with this request. The context object may or may not be defined as part of an operation in an interface definition, so it may not appear in the method for a given operation.

❹ This line indicates the `job_class` argument. This argument is specific to this particular request and is a single character denoting the job classification of the employee being hired.

### 9.4.6.1 Creating an Object Reference

Sometimes your method needs to create object references. For example, the method that actually does the work of hiring an employee needs to create an object reference for the newly hired employee so that employee can be represented in the company's computer systems.

You use the `CORBA_BOA_create` operation to create an object reference. When an object reference is created, the real-world object is entered into the CORBA system and is associated with both an interface and an implementation. To preserve the client's separation from how a server actually accomplishes the client's request, the `CORBA_BOA_create` operation should be used only by a server and not by a client.

Example 9–3 shows the use of the `CORBA_BOA_create` operation to create an object reference for the newly hired employee.

**Example 9–3  Creating an Object Reference**

```
/* C */

CORBA_ReferenceData  ref_data;
.
.
.
```

(continued on next page)

**Example 9–3 (Cont.) Creating an Object Reference**

```
ref_data . _maximum = sizeof(void *);
ref_data . _length = sizeof(void *);
ref_data . _buffer = (CORBA_octet *) &employeeKey;
CORBA_BOA_create    ( CORBA_vendor_BOA_OBJECT, ❶
                       ev,                      ❷
                       & ref_data,              ❸
                       NewEmployeeIntfcObj,     ❹
                       NewEmployeeImplObj );     ❺
 .
 .
 .
}
```

❶ This line shows the use of the CORBA_BOA_create operation to identify the object reference for the newly hired employee.

❷ This line specifies the environment argument that can contain exception information related to the object reference.

❸ This line shows the reference data associated with the object reference being created.

❹ This line specifies the interface repository object that contains the complete set of interfaces implemented by the object.

❺ This line specifies the implementation repository object that contains the implementation to be used by the object being referenced.

For more detailed information on using the CORBA_BOA_create operation and specific information on how an interface is bound to an implementation using this operation, see Chapter 10.

### 9.4.6.2 Disposing of an Object Reference

Just as your methods might need to create an object reference, your methods will probably need to delete those object references. You use the CORBA_BOA_dispose operation to delete object references.

As with CORBA_BOA_create, only code on the server should delete object references because using the CORBA_BOA_dispose operation actually removes an object and all its associated data from the system. Because the client does not own the object, it should not be the one to dispose of it. You should only use the CORBA_BOA_dispose operation when the actual object no longer exists, such as when an employee leaves the company.

If you need to free the memory associated with an object reference for a client or a server and you do not want to delete that object from the system, you should use the CORBA_Object_release operation and not the CORBA_BOA_dispose operation.

### 9.4.6.3 Getting Data About an Object

If your methods need to get information about the real-world object represented by an object reference, you should use the CORBA_BOA_get_id operation.

When an object reference is created, one of the arguments to the CORBA_BOA_create operation is the reference data associated with the object reference being created. CORBA does not define what is contained in this reference data, but typically it contains information that uniquely identifies the object for which the object reference is being created, such as a pathname to a specific file, or a key into a database.

Example 9–4 shows the use of the CORBA_BOA_get_id operation.

**Example 9–4   C Mapping for Getting Reference Data**

```
/* C */
CORBA_ReferenceData      ref_data;
.
.
.
ref_data = CORBA_BOA_get_id( CORBA_vendor_BOA_OBJECT, ❶
                            ev,
                            object );
employee = (* (EmployeeKey **) ref_data . _buffer );
CORBA_free( ref_data . _buffer ); ❷
```

❶ This line shows the CORBA_BOA_get_id operation to get the reference data from the object reference. The object reference itself is opaque and may be different for different ORBs, but the id value is available portably in all ORBs. Only the implementation can normally interpret the id value.

❷ This line shows the CORBA_free routine, which releases all memory associated with the reference data.

### 9.4.6.4 Signaling an Exception

Exception information is stored in the environment argument to a request. When an exception occurs in a method as a result of an operation not being performed successfully, you place that information in the environment argument using the CORBA_BOA_set_exception operation. This is referred to as "raising an exception." The method can raise only standard exceptions or any user-defined exceptions that are defined for the requested operation.

If there is no problem with the operation, there is usually no need to explicitly set the exception type to the CORBA_NO_EXCEPTION constant. Most vendors set this exception type for you in the BOA, but before relying on it, you should verify that this is the case with your CORBA system. If your CORBA vendor does not set the CORBA_NO_EXCEPTION constant for you, then you will need to do it yourself in your server.

If there is an exception, your method needs to raise it and you need to write code to decide what to do with the method when this error occurs. For example, you might decide that it is a trivial error and continue, or you might decide to have the method terminate and clean up any resources it had used.

Example 9–5 shows the C mapping for the CORBA_BOA_set_exception operation.

**Example 9–5  C Mapping for Raising an Exception**

```
/* C */
CORBA_void CORBA_BOA_set_exception(BOA, ev, major, exceptionname, params)

CORBA_Object          BOA;              ❶
CORBA_Environment     *ev;              ❷
CORBA_Exception_type  major;            ❸
CORBA_char            *exceptionname;   ❹
CORBA_void            *params;          ❺
```

To raise an exception, you must do the following:

❶ Specify the object of the operation; in this case, it is the CORBA vendor's BOA object.

❷ Specify the environment argument to contain any exception information associated with the processing of this operation.

❸ Set the major argument to the constant that represents the kind of exception you are raising. Set it to the CORBA_SYSTEM_EXCEPTION constant for a standard exception or to the CORBA_USER_EXCEPTION constant for a user-defined exception.

❹ Set the exceptionname argument to the character string that identifies the exception.

❺ If the exception that is being raised has any parameters associated with it, then set the params argument to the address of the structure that contains those parameters, and cast that argument as a CORBA_void * argument.

Example 9–6 shows the standard exception, Unknown, raised by a method coded in C.

**Example 9–6   C Mapping for Raising a Standard Exception**

```
/* C */
CORBA_BOA_set_exception
    (
    CORBA_Vendor_BOA_OBJECT, ❶
    ev, ❷
    CORBA_SYSTEM_EXCEPTION, ❸
    ex_CORBA_UNKNOWN, ❹
    (CORBA_void *)&body ❺
    );
```

❶ This line shows the BOA object being specified. Each CORBA vendor has a different BOA; in this example, we're using the name CORBA_Vendor_BOA_OBJECT to indicate a particular vendor's BOA.

❷ This line shows the environment argument as indicated by the ev variable in which information relating to an exception raised as a result of this operation would be stored.

❸ This line shows the constant for the kind of exception being raised; in this case, CORBA_SYSTEM_EXCEPTION indicates that a standard exception is being raised.

❹ This line shows that the character string identifier for the exception being raised is ex_CORBA_UNKNOWN, which corresponds to the Unknown standard exception.

❺ This line shows the address of the structure, &body, being passed in. This structure contains the parameters associated with the Unknown standard exception. Note that this argument is cast to be CORBA_void *.

### 9.4.6.5 Handling Authentication and Access Control

CORBA does not specify any particular authentication or access control scheme. If you need to handle authentication or access control in the methods in your server application, you will either use those provided by your CORBA vendor or add those capabilities yourself. One way that your CORBA vendor can supply you with authentication and access control capabilities is through the use of the `CORBA_BOA_get_principal` operation.

The `CORBA_BOA_get_principal` operation allows you to obtain the identity of the issuer of a request for an operation. This information can be used for authentication or access control and is stored in the **principal object**. The principal object describes the identity of the individual who issued the request through whatever authentication, access control, or other security information your vendor's CORBA system places there. What exactly is in the principal object will depend on the security environment your CORBA vendor has supplied.

For example, suppose that before a method does its work, it must verify that the issuer of the request is authorized to make this request. The method would use the `CORBA_BOA_get_principal` operation to get this information from the principal object to authenticate the issuer of the request.

CORBA provides the principal object and the `CORBA_BOA_get_principal` operation defined on that object as a hook to allow vendors to provide their own security schemes as part of their CORBA systems. The principal object is not a complete security facility; it is only a starting point for building security and access control mechanisms into a CORBA system.

The OMG is planning a much richer, common security service. However, for now, you must use whatever you or your vendor can provide.

### 9.4.6.6 Switching Implementations for an Object Reference

The `CORBA_BOA_change_implementation` operation allows you to change the implementation associated with an object reference so that all subsequent requests using that object reference will use the new implementation. However, you should avoid using this operation in most circumstances. In fact, the CORBA specification contains a note that explains why you should use this operation cautiously:

> "Care must be taken in order to change the implementation after the object has been created. There are issues of synchronization with activation, security, and whether or not the new implementation is prepared to handle requests for that object."

### 9.4.7 Creating Initial Object References

The problem of creating the first objects to be used by clients to make requests tends to be handled by server applications. Both clients and servers need objects to begin their work in a CORBA system; servers need the actual objects themselves and clients need references to those objects. However, CORBA does not specify how to create these objects and object references. Typically, CORBA server applications will create object references at installation either by using some utility provided by the CORBA vendor or by executing a server in some special installation-only mode.

Once created at installation, these object references are stored in some persistent fashion so they can be used whenever the clients or servers are started. For example, these object references can be stored as string-formatted objects in data files or as entries in a name service or registry.

# 10

# Associating the Client Operation with the Server Method

In Chapters 8 and 9, we explained how to create a CORBA client and server, respectively. In this chapter, we explain how a client is associated with a server. By understanding some of the ways this association can be made, you can better understand the flexibility of various CORBA systems and how much flexibility you might need in this area for your own CORBA-based application or framework.

We begin by discussing the CORBA_BOA_create operation, which associates the client interface with the server implementation. We will then look at how various CORBA systems might make this association and when a CORBA system actually does the mapping.

## 10.1 The CORBA_BOA_create Operation

An operation that a client can request is defined on an object that is defined by an interface. Similarly, a method is defined as part of an implementation in a server. An interface is associated with an implementation when the server performs the CORBA_BOA_create operation.

The only reason to use the CORBA_BOA_create operation is to create an object reference for a client to use to make a request on that object. That request for an operation causes a method to perform the task requested. When you create an object reference using CORBA_BOA_create, that object reference is associated with an interface definition and an implementation definition. This is shown in the C binding of the CORBA_BOA_create operation in Example 10–1. The interface definition, intf, describes a specific interface that describes the operations a client can request. The implementation definition, impl, describes a specific implementation that, in turn, describes the implementations (and within them the methods) available to perform a client operation.

**Example 10–1  Using the CORBA_BOA_create Operation**

```
/* C */
Object CORBA_BOA_create ❶
    (
    Object           boa, ❷
    Environment      *ev, ❸
    ReferenceData    *refdata, ❹
    InterfaceDef     intf, ❺
    ImplementationDef impl ❻
    );
```

❶ The CORBA_BOA_create operation returns the object reference being created.

❷ The object for this operation is the BOA object, boa, because this is the object on which the create operation is defined.

❸ The environment argument.

❹ The reference data associated with the object reference being created. The reference data can contain anything, but most typically it contains information that uniquely defines the object being created, such as a filepath or a key into a database.

❺ The interface definition object that specifies the interface supported by the object being referenced. You might get this object by retrieving it from the interface repository or through some other means.

❻ The implementation definition object that specifies the implementation to be used by the object being referenced. You might get this object by retrieving it from the implementation repository or through some other means.

## 10.2  How Vendors Map Interfaces to Implementations

When you first look at the arguments to the CORBA_BOA_create operation, there appears to be a one-to-one mapping between an interface and an implementation; however, this is not necessarily the case.

CORBA specifies that an InterfaceDef and an ImplementationDef object should exist and be accessible through an interface repository and an implementation repository, respectively. It also specifies several OMG IDL operations that can be used to retrieve information from an InterfaceDef object. However, that is all that CORBA says regarding these objects; the remaining details, such as their forms, are left to each CORBA vendor

to determine in the context of their own systems. It is because the
ImplementationDef object reference is so vendor specific that there can be
some variation in how an interface is actually mapped to an implementation.

Some CORBA vendors might implement a one-to-one mapping between an
interface and an implementation. Others, however, might view this mapping
as too restrictive. These vendors might build their systems to offer an interface
a choice of implementations (or even multiple implementations) or to defer the
association of implementation to interface until run time.

The following sections examine some of the ways that CORBA vendors map an
interface to an implementation.

## 10.2.1 The Simple Case: One Interface to One Implementation

Some CORBA vendors might build their systems to support one implementation per interface. In this simplest case, there is a one-to-one
relationship between the operations in the interface and the methods in
the implementation, as shown in Figure 10–1.

**Figure 10–1  One Implementation Per Interface**

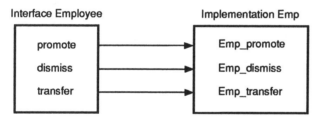

ZK-7737A

You can see that the promote, dismiss, and transfer operations on the
Employee interface are mapped to the Emp_promote, Emp_dismiss, and
Emp_transfer methods in the Emp implementation.

Although this approach has the advantage of being simple, it is also fairly
inflexible because each operation must be supported by a method in the
implementation; the operations and methods must match each other exactly.
Adding a new operation to the interface used by the client would require
adding a matching method to the implementation. This inflexibility can
force you to write interface definitions that are too closely tied to how those
interfaces are implemented, which results in a lack of separation between your
clients and servers.

## 10.2.2 More Flexible: One Interface to One of Many Implementations

Other CORBA vendors might build their systems to be more flexible and support one of several implementations for one interface. There is still a one-to-one relationship between the interface operations and the methods in the implementations; however, you can have several implementations. To make these implementations unique, some vendors might require that different implementations that support the same interface be deployed on different host machines or in different servers. Figure 10–2 illustrates this approach.

**Figure 10–2  Many Implementations Per Interface**

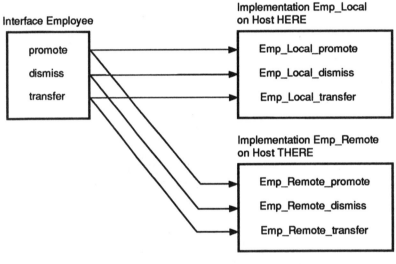

ZK-7738A

Allowing multiple implementations gives you the flexibility to have different, but similar, implementations for the same interface. However, this approach still requires operations and methods to match each other exactly; changing one will affect the other.

In this example, the promote, dismiss, and transfer operations on the Employee interface can be mapped to either the Emp_Remote or the Emp_Local implementations. In our example, the Emp_Remote implementation uses the remote centralized employee database to get its employee information. Although this database is physically far away, it contains the most up-to-date information. The Emp_Local implementation uses the local employee database to get its employee information. This database is a local copy of the centralized employee database. This local database is updated once a week from the centralized database and tends to be current enough for employee-related data that does not change often.

Of course, now that more than one implementation could possibly match the interface, some mechanism for selecting one implementation over another is needed. Some vendors might use information in the context object as the basis for determining which implementation to use; some might use a form of a name service, and others might use information that is stored in the system some other way.

In this example, the context object passed with the request specifies that the operation requires the latest data. Therefore, the operation is associated with the Emp_Remote implementation because the request cannot be satisfied by the Emp_Local implementation, which might contain outdated information.

## 10.2.3 Most Flexible: One Interface to Multiple Implementations

Other CORBA vendors might build their systems to allow multiple implementations to be associated with the same interface, with each implementation providing only a portion of the interface. This idea of spreading an interface across several implementations is called **implementation spreading**.

Figure 10–3 illustrates implementation spreading and shows how several implementations can be used to support a single interface. In this example, the Employee interface supports the promote, dismiss, and transfer operations. The Manager interface supports these same operations plus the approve_transfer operation.

With implementation spreading, one implementation, such as Common_Emp, can contain all the methods that map to the operations the two interfaces have in common, and another implementation, such as App_Tran, can contain only the method necessary to carry out the approve_transfer operation. Without implementation spreading, we would need two separate implementations that would both contain the methods to perform the three operations that these two interfaces have in common.

Implementation spreading allows you to reuse existing methods rather than duplicate them in another implementation. This makes the code easier to maintain because the methods exist in one place only.

**Figure 10–3  Multiple Implementations Per Interface**

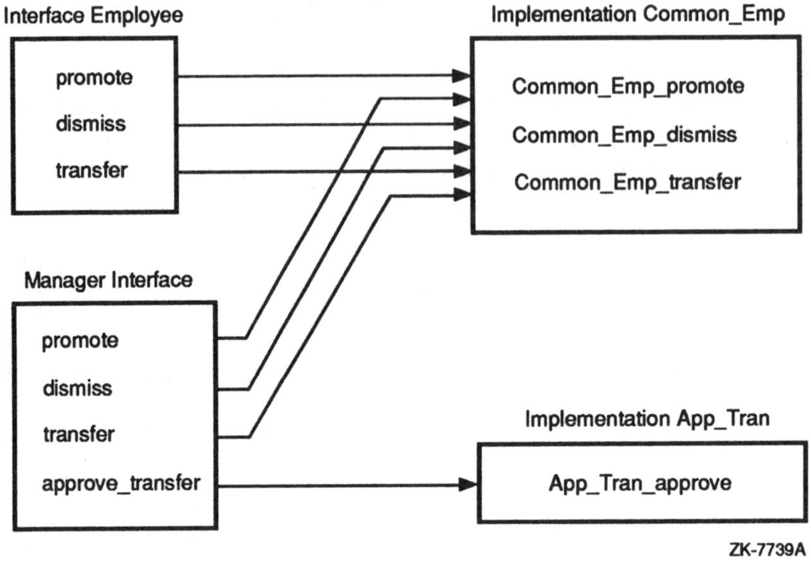

Interface Employee

```
promote
dismiss
transfer
```

Implementation Common_Emp

```
Common_Emp_promote
Common_Emp_dismiss
Common_Emp_transfer
```

Manager Interface

```
promote
dismiss
transfer
approve_transfer
```

Implementation App_Tran

```
App_Tran_approve
```

ZK-7739A

Implementation spreading allows the mapping of operations to methods, rather than the mapping of interfaces to implementations. Implementation spreading allows you to spread the methods that are needed to support an interface across several implementations. When using implementation spreading, you will probably want to group related methods into the same implementations. By mapping an interface to a single implementation, that implementation must support all operations of the interface. For example, suppose the employee interface had over a dozen different operations available to it. Without implementation spreading, all the methods to support those operations would have to be in the same implementation. With implementation spreading, those methods can be divided into logical subgroups of implementations and spread across several servers or hosts.

## 10.3  When the Association Occurs

We have discussed the ways that a CORBA vendor could associate an interface with an implementation, but have not discussed when that association might take place. This, too, is an area where CORBA systems differ.

The actual association between a particular interface and a particular implementation can occur anytime after you create the object reference using the CORBA_BOA_create operation, up to the point of making a request. Although the association can be made at any time, it is useful to think of the association as being either an early binding or a late binding. These terms are not part of CORBA, but they are helpful distinctions.

With early binding, the ImplementationDef argument to the CORBA_BOA_create operation indicates a specific implementation. When the object reference is returned from that operation, you have all the information you need to use that implementation, although that information could be stored not only in the object reference, but also somewhere else in the system, such as in the object adapter. Early binding tends to be used when the CORBA system uses one interface to one implementation mapping.

With late binding, the ImplementationDef argument to the CORBA_BOA_create operation is not a specific implementation, but can be some kind of variable that represents several implementations or indicates that an implementation should not be chosen until the request is actually invoked. Late binding tends to be used when the CORBA system supports the use of one interface to one of several implementations or one interface to multiple implementations. Late binding of interfaces to implementations allows more flexibility than early binding, because the implementation selection process is postponed, allowing additional information, such as user preferences, to be considered when selecting the implementation best suited to map to an interface.

When you use late binding and have the object reference returned from the CORBA_BOA_create operation, that object reference cannot contain all the information needed to select an implementation; some other resolution process needs to be used to get a specific implementation. For example, the variable ImplementationDef cannot be filled in with a specific implementation until a request using the object reference is actually made. At that time, certain information available to the system allows the system to select the best implementation.

CORBA vendors who use late binding will establish criteria for determining which implementation to select. Some late binding vendors might use information known primarily by the client, such as the information in the context object; others might use information known primarily by the object adapter (and private to the object adapter). Such information could be stored in the context object, the object adapter, or somewhere in the ORB itself.

Once an implementation is selected, it needs to be validated to make sure it exists in the system and supports the associated interface. In some CORBA systems, when an implementation is selected, a server might be also selected as part of that implementation. This is typically because only one implementation of a certain kind is allowed.

However, other CORBA vendors might allow the selection of a server for the implementation when multiple servers with the same kind of implementation are available. Again, this ability to select a server apart from the selection of an implementation offers more flexibility in designing the implementations and servers in your application or framework.

# Part IV

## Deploying a CORBA Application into a CORBA System

Part IV is written for both the application developer and the application designer. This part discusses the issues pertaining to the deployment of a distributed application or framework and the deployment of an application within a vendor's CORBA system or framework.

Deploying an application is the process of placing an application in a distributed environment and making it available for use. **Deployment** can include such tasks as installation, configuration, and administration of various parts of the application.

We will refer to decisions we need to make to deploy our personnel example application as examples of the issues that you might have to consider with other applications.

# 11

## Deploying the Application

Deploying an application (or framework) is the process of packaging it so that the right parts are installed in the right places. Because CORBA systems vary a great deal between vendors, our approach here is more along the lines of "things to consider" rather than detailed instructions. First, we will consider some general deployment topics, then topics related to deploying the client and the server.

## 11.1 General Deployment Considerations

The following are some general topics to consider when deploying your distributed CORBA-based application or framework.

### 11.1.1 Determining Which Client and Server Platforms to Support

You might not want, or need, to support all the client and server platforms that your CORBA vendor supports. For example, if you need a single server platform but you want multiple client platforms, you might decide to support all the client platforms that your CORBA vendor supports, but only one of the server platforms.

### 11.1.2 Determining How to Package Kits

In CORBA, an application can be only a client, only a server, or a client and server. Accordingly, you can package your distributed application as a client-only kit, a server-only kit, a combined client and server kit, or all three, with each kit available on various platforms.

If possible, consider how to package your kits when designing and developing your application. Thinking about how you can subdivide and sell your product early in the design process will make building the installation kits for your finished product significantly easier.

For example, if you decide during the design phase to sell a client-only package, you can design and build the client portion of your distributed application as a modular piece that is easily separated from the rest of the system. If you make this decision after the distributed application is completed, you might need to change the application to separate the client from the rest of the system, which could prove very difficult to do.

### 11.1.3 Tips For Your Installation Procedure

The following are some tips for features to put into your installation procedure:

- Standardize where you install your files if the CORBA system or framework does not.

  If your CORBA system or framework does not define a standard place in which to install certain files or repositories, use your installation procedure to suggest or enforce such standard locations. For example, your installation procedure could suggest that the interface and implementation repositories be installed in the CORBA system or product root directory.

  You can also have your installation procedure look for certain files on the system to see where other distributed applications have installed files and place your files in the same area.

- Create a distributed test program that verifies your installation.

  As part of the installation procedure, you should include a program that verifies whether your distributed components can send and receive requests to and from each other. Ideally, such a program should send and receive simple requests from all installed clients and servers.

  Testing the capabilities of only the clients or the servers is not sufficient in a distributed environment because those tests do not check to see if the clients and servers can communicate with each other. Even if your kit is a server-only or client-only kit, you should still make sure your newly installed clients or servers can communicate with the rest of the system.

- Check that the CORBA system is installed.

  As part of the installation procedure for your distributed application, check the version of the CORBA system already installed. Once you have verified that the CORBA system is installed, you can assume that any prerequisite software the CORBA system requires is also installed. This checking simplifies your installation by reducing the number of types and configurations of software (networks, platforms) you have to check for.

### 11.1.4 Invocation Issues in Deploying a Framework

If you are building a distributed framework, the openness of your framework partially determines whether or not you need provide the interface definitions and influences the invocation type.

For example, if you have an open framework that allows you to add and change applications within it, then you need to supply your interface definitions in some form so that they can be included in your new applications. The client side of new applications will need the interface definitions for using stub-style or dynamic invocation; the server side will need the interface definitions to generate server skeletons. One example of such a framework is a software engineering environment with a changing set of compilers, debuggers, editors, and class libraries.

On the other hand, if you have a closed framework that contains all the applications that are ever going to be part of the framework, then you do not need to supply your interface definitions because there will be no new applications that will need them. However, if you do not include the interface definitions, you will also not be able to use dynamic invocation, which depends on those interface definitions being available in the interface repository. An example of such a framework is one that by legal contract is designed to not change over the course of a complex project, such as building a submarine or a city planning project.

## 11.2 Deploying a CORBA-Based Client

Client deployment includes deploying any application-specific data or executable files that are part of your client application, such as deploying your interface definitions or deploying the stubs used for stub-style invocation.

### 11.2.1 Getting Object References for the Client

To send a request, a client first needs to get an object reference on which to make the request; but, to get an object reference, the client needs to send a request that returns an object reference. Because clients do not create objects or object references, each CORBA vendor must supply a mechanism that clients can use to obtain the an object reference they need to get started.

One way to provide these object references is to deploy previously created object references with the client. These object references could be in a file, in some kind of database, or in a name service or registry. When the client application is started, it retrieves these object references to use in sending requests. The responses to these requests can then provide the rest of the object references that the client application needs to do its work.

### 11.2.2 Deploying Interface Definitions

If your client supports only stub-style invocation, it is possible that you do not actually need to deploy your interface definitions, although that will depend on how your CORBA system is set up. If you need to deploy your interface definitions, then you need to decide how to do it. When interface definitions are coded in OMG IDL, you can deploy the OMG IDL files and then load them into an interface repository.

If your CORBA system supports multiple interface repositories, you can also deploy an interface repository with the interface definition files already loaded into it. However, it is generally best to deploy the OMG IDL, then load it into the interface repository. When you install interface definitions that are already loaded into your own interface repository, you will create another interface repository on the system and you will be depending on your CORBA system's ability to support multiple interface repositories. In addition, even if multiple interface repositories are supported, you will be adding what is probably unnecessary complexity to setting up, running, and maintaining your application or framework.

### 11.2.3 Choosing a Format in Which to Deploy Client Stubs

If you are supporting stub-style invocation and your CORBA vendor allows you to generate stubs in source format, you can ship your stubs as source code or as precompiled object code.

In most cases, you should probably ship your client stubs as source code, not object code. Shipping client stubs as object code could become a logistical nightmare because you would have to generate that object code for whatever linkers are available on the hardware and software platforms you support. If you ship the stubs in source format, you will need to worry much less about which linker is installed on the system on which you are deploying your client because your stubs will be compiled and linked on site with matching versions of the compiler and linker.

## 11.3 Deploying a CORBA-Based Server

Server deployment includes installing the implementations and methods that make up those implementations, installing any application-specific data or executable files that are part of your server application, and installing the server skeletons used to connect the object adapter to the implementations.

### 11.3.1 Creating and Distributing Objects with the Server

Getting an object for your server is the same problem the client has in getting object references. Many vendors provide a reference to the BOA object to allow the server to begin its work using the operations defined on the BOA, such as CORBA_BOA_create.

Once the server is running, it might need to supply objects to other server applications or object references to client applications. To do this, the server must generate the objects, for example, by using a vendor-supplied utility.

Once created, the server might need to place the objects and object references where the servers and clients can access them. It is likely that the CORBA vendor will supply this access mechanism. You might need to deploy certain parts of this access mechanism along with your server (for example, any files used to store the objects or object references).

### 11.3.2 Deploying Implementation Definitions

When you deploy your implementation definitions onto your server, your CORBA vendor might have provided an implementation repository to load them into. CORBA defines an implementation repository, but it does not specify how that repository is used or by whom, the form of an implementation repository, or how it is accessed. Therefore, the implementation repository very likely differs among CORBA systems. An implementation repository could be as simple as a directory in which the implementation objects and definitions are files or as sophisticated as an object-oriented database that contains definitions of each of the objects.

If your CORBA vendor does not supply an implementation repository, it will supply some other mechanism for storing and retrieving implementation definitions. Regardless of whether there is an implementation repository, you need to somehow deploy your implementation definitions so the system can find the implementations it needs to activate.

### 11.3.3 Deploying Persistent Servers

If you install a persistent server, that server needs to be activated as soon as the CORBA system itself is activated. The procedure to activate persistent servers varies among CORBA systems. For example, if the persistent servers in your CORBA system are started using scripts, then as part of the deployment of your persistent server, you need to install a script to start your server and perhaps call it from the system startup file as well.

# A
# Extended Code Examples

This appendix collects the code examples used throughout this book and shows them in their entirety. Note that these code examples are only coding fragments and are not working applications.

## A.1 Example OMG IDL for Personnel Objects and Operations in Module CORP.IDL

This example focuses on the operations used by a personnel administrator to hire employees and maintain information about employees within a corporation. This is not meant to be a full-featured example, but instead is meant to show some important object-oriented concepts in general, and some important CORBA concepts, specifically.

In Example A–1, the module CORP is used to group the corporate-wide interfaces and to illustrate that it is recommended to contain all related interfaces within a module so as to avoid name clashes between other service groups or organizations within your corporation or enterprise. The module ENGINEERING is used to group the engineering interfaces and to illustrate inheritance from the CORP module.

The OMG IDL shown in this example is used to illustrate various design and OMG IDL coding points in this book. See Chapter 4 for more information on designing a set of CORBA interface definitions for a distributed application.

### Example A–1  CORP.IDL Interface Definitions

```
/* Corporate Applications OMG IDL source file
   File:  CORP.IDL  */

module CORP
{
// Forward declaration for interfaces
    interface Employee;

// Declarations of variables used throughout this module
    typedef long            BadgeNum;
    typedef long            DeptNum;
    enum DismissalCode      { DISMISS_FIRED, DISMISS_QUIT };
    enum DenyApprovalReasons  { REASON,CODES };

    exception DENY_APPROVAL
        {
        DenyApprovalReasons  reason;
        };

// Declarations of data for data types
    struct PersonalData
        {
        string              last_name;
        string              first_name;
        string              middle_name;
        string              phone;
        string              site;
        };
    typedef PersonalData EmpPersonalData;
    struct EmpData
        {
        BadgeNum            id;
        EmpPersonalData     personal_info;
        char                job_class;
        float               hourly_rate;
        };

    struct DeptInfo
        {
        DeptNum             id;
        string              name;
        };

// Interface Definitions
    interface Department                    // forward declaration
        {
                attribute DeptInfo              DeptID;
        readonly attribute Employee            manager_obj;
        }; // end of interface Department
```

(continued on next page)

**Example A–1 (Cont.) CORP.IDL Interface Definitions**

```
interface Employee
    {
            attribute EmpData            personal_data;
    readonly attribute Department        department_obj;
    void promote    ( in   char          new_job_class );
    void dismiss    ( in   DismissalCode  reason,
                      in   string         description);
    void transfer   ( in   Department     new_dept_obj);
    }; // end of interface Employee

interface Manager : Employee
    {
    void approve_transfer ( in  Employee      employee_obj,
                            in  Department     current_department,
                            in  Department     new_department)
                            raises (DENY_APPROVAL)
                            context ("division");
    }; // end of interface Manager

interface Personnel : Employee
    {
    Employee hire ( in  EmpData       employee_data,
                    in  Department     department_obj,
                    out BadgeNum       new_employee_id);
    }; // end of interface Personnel

interface PersonnelManager : Personnel, Manager
    {
    void arbitrate ( );
    }; // end of interface PersonnelManager
}; //end of module CORP

module ENGINEERING
{
// Interface Definitions
    interface EmployeeLocator
        {
        void FindEngineer ( in  CORP::BadgeNum      id,
                            out CORP::PersonalData   info);
        };
    interface PersonnelManager : CORP::PersonnelManager
        {
        };
}; // end module ENGINEERING
```

## A.2 Example C Code for the Client Application

Example A–2 shows a client application that supports the hire operation on the Personnel object as it was defined using the interfaces in CORP.IDL (shown in Example A–1).

Example A–2 shows the code for our sample client application. The client application accepts the name of an employee as input from an end user and then requests a hire operation on that employee.

See Chapter 8 for more information on developing a CORBA client application.

**Example A–2  Example Client Application, Client_main.C**

```
/* C */

/* Client_main.c  sample personnel client application */

/* Standard C include files */
#include <stdio.h>
#include <stdlib.h>

/* Include typedefs and so on generated from CORP.IDL */
#include "CORP.h"

/* Begin Main client program */

main (int argc, char ** argv)
{
 /* Declarations */

 CORBA_Object          pers_obj;      /* Personnel object */
 CORBA_Object          dep_obj;       /* Department object */
 CORBA_Object          emp_obj;       /* Employee object */
 CORBA_Status          status;
 CORBA_Environment      ev;
 FILE                  * temp_file;
 CORBA_char            string_obj [1024];
 CORP_EmpData          emp_data;
 CORP_BadgeNum         badge_num;

 /*.....................................................*/
```

(continued on next page)

**Example A–2 (Cont.)  Example Client Application, Client_main.C**

```
/* Get employee information from the end user */
if (argc < 7)
    {
    fprintf(stderr,
            "Usage : %s department last first middle class rate\n",
            argv[0]);
    exit(0);
    }
/* Get the Personnel object from the file */
temp_file = fopen("PersFile.dat", "r");
if (temp_file == NULL)
    {
    fprintf(stderr,
            "Could not open file to get Personnel object reference\n",
            argv[1]);
    exit(0);
    }
if (fgets(string_obj, sizeof(string_obj), temp_file) == NULL)
    {
    fprintf(stderr,
            "Could not read the Personnel object from the file\n");
    exit(0);
    }
fclose(temp_file);

/* Convert the string-formatted Personnel object reference to a binary-formatted
   object reference */

pers_obj = CORBA_ORB_string_to_object (
                                CORBA_Vendor_ORB_OBJECT,
                                & ev,
                                string_obj);

if (ev . _major != CORBA_NO_EXCEPTION || pers_obj == (CORBA_Object) NULL)
    {
    CORBA_exception_free( & ev );
    CORBA_Object_release(pers_obj, & ev);
    Vendor_ORB_rundown( CORBA_Vendor_ORB_OBJECT,
                        (CORBA_Environment *)NULL,
                        (CORBA_Flags)0 );
    exit(0);
    }
```

(continued on next page)

**Example A–2 (Cont.)  Example Client Application, Client_main.C**

```
/* Get the Department object from the file using the employee name passed in */
temp_file = fopen(argv[1], "r");
if (temp_file == NULL)
    {
    fprintf(stderr,
            "Could not open File %s to get Department object reference\n",
            argv[1]);
    exit(0);
    }
if (fgets(string_obj, sizeof(string_obj), temp_file) == NULL)
    {
    fprintf(stderr,
            "Could not read the Department object reference from the file\n");
    exit(0);
    }
fclose(temp_file);

/* Convert the string-formatted Department object reference to a binary-formatted
   object reference */

dep_obj = CORBA_ORB_string_to_object (
                            CORBA_Vendor_ORB_OBJECT,
                            & ev,
                            string_obj);

if (ev . _major != CORBA_NO_EXCEPTION || dep_obj == (CORBA_Object) NULL)
    {
    CORBA_exception_free( & ev );
    CORBA_Object_release(dep_obj, & ev);
    Vendor_ORB_rundown( CORBA_Vendor_ORB_OBJECT,
                        (CORBA_Environment *)NULL,
                        (CORBA_Flags)0 );
    exit(0);
    ;

/* Fill out the emp_data argument */
emp_data . last_name = argv[2];
emp_data . first_name = argv[3];
emp_data . middle_name = argv[4];
emp_data . job_class = * argv[5];
emp_data . hourly_rate = atof(argv[6]);
```

(continued on next page)

**Example A–2 (Cont.)  Example Client Application, Client_main.C**

```
/* Hire the employee */
emp_obj = CORP_Personnel_hire(pers_obj, &ev, &emp_data, dep_obj, & badge_num);
if (ev . _major != CORBA_NO_EXCEPTION)
    {
    printf("Could not hire the employee\n");
    CORBA_exception_free( & ev );
    CORBA_Object_release(dep_obj, & ev);
    CORBA_Object_release(pers_obj, & ev);
    Vendor_ORB_rundown( CORBA_Vendor_ORB_OBJECT,
                        (CORBA_Environment *)NULL,
                        (CORBA_Flags)0 );
    exit( 0 );
    }
/* Get the employee's data to verify the data is correct */
emp_data = CORP_Employee_get_EmpData(emp_obj, &ev);
if (ev . _major != CORBA_NO_EXCEPTION)
    {
    fprintf(stderr,"Could not get the employee data \n");
    CORBA_exception_free( & ev );
    CORBA_Object_release(emp_obj, & ev);
    CORBA_Object_release(dep_obj, & ev);
    CORBA_Object_release(pers_obj, & ev);
    Vendor_ORB_rundown( CORBA_Vendor_ORB_OBJECT,
                        (CORBA_Environment *)NULL,
                        (CORBA_Flags)0 );
    exit(0);
    }
/* Echo the employee data back to the end user */
printf("Hiring process complete for employee:\n");
printf("\tLast Name : \t%s\n", emp_data . last_name);
printf("\tFirst Name : \t%s\n", emp_data . first_name);
printf("\tMiddle Name : \t%s\n", emp_data . middle_name);
printf("\tJob Class : \t%c\n", emp_data . job_class);
printf("\tHourly Rate: %f\n", emp_data . hourly_rate);

/* Release all memory associated with emp_data argument */
CORBA_free(emp_data . last_name);
CORBA_free(emp_data . first_name);
CORBA_free(emp_data . middle_name);
```

(continued on next page)

**Example A–2 (Cont.)  Example Client Application, Client_main.C**

```
/* Release all the objects */
CORBA_Object_release(emp_obj, & ev);
CORBA_Object_release(dep_obj, & ev);
CORBA_Object_release(pers_obj, & ev);
if (ev . _major != CORBA_NO_EXCEPTION)
exit(0);
} /* end of main */
```

# A.3  Example C++ Code for the Client Application

Example A–3 shows a client application coded in C++ that supports the hire operation on the Personnel object as it was defined using the interfaces in CORP.IDL (shown in Example A–1).

Example A–3 shows the code for our sample client application. The client application accepts the name of an employee as input from an end user and then requests a hire operation on that employee.

See Chapter 8 for more information on developing a CORBA client application.

**Example A–3  Example Client Application, Client_main.cxx**

```
// CXX

// Client_main.cxx  sample personnel client application

// C++ stream definitions
#include <iostream.h>
#include <fstream.h>

// Include typedefs and so on generated from CORP.IDL
#include "CORP.hxx"

OBB::ORB * CORBA_Vendor_ORB;

// Begin Main client program

main (int argc, char ** argv)
{
  /* Declarations */
```

(continued on next page)

**xample A–3 (Cont.)  Example Client Application, Client_main.cxx**

```
CORBA::Object_ptr        pers_obj_ptr;
CORBA::Object_ptr        dep_obj_ptr;
ORP::Personnel_var       pers_obj;        // Personnel object
ORP::Department_var      dep_obj;         // Department object
ORP::Employee_var        emp_obj;         // Employee object

CORBA::Status            status;
CORBA::Environment       ev;
fstream  temp_file;
har                      string_obj [1024];
ORP::EmpData             emp_data;
ORP::BadgeNum            badge_num;

. . . . . . . . . . . . . . . . . . . . . . . . . . . . . . . . . . . . . . . . . . . . . . . .

/ Get employee information from the end user
f (argc < 7)
    {
    cerr << "Usage : " << argv[0] <<
  " department last first middle class rate" << endl;
    exit(0);
    }
/ Get the Personnel object from the file
emp_file . open ("PersFile.dat", ios::in);
f (!temp_file)
    {
    cerr << "Could not open file to get Personnel object reference" <<
      endl;
    exit(0);
    }
emp_file >> string_obj;
f (!temp_file)
    {
    cerr << "Could not read the Personnel object from the file" <<
      endl;
    exit(0);
    }
emp_file . close();

/ Convert the string-formatted Personnel object reference to a
/ binary-formatted CORBA::Object reference

ers_obj_ptr = CORBA_Vendor_ORB -> string_to_object (
                                    string_obj,
                                    ev);
```

(continued on next page)

**Example A–3 (Cont.)  Example Client Application, Client_main.cxx**

```
if ((ev . exception()) || (CORBA::is_nil(pers_obj_ptr, ev)))
    {
    ev . clear();
    CORBA::release (pers_obj_ptr, ev );
    CORBA_Vendor_ORB -> rundown ((CORBA::Flags) 0, ev);
    exit(0);
    }

// Narrow the CORBA::Object to a CORP::Personnel object reference
pers_obj = CORP::Personnel::_narrow(pers_obj_ptr);

if (!pers_obj)
    {
    ev . clear();
    CORBA::release (pers_obj_ptr, ev );
    CORBA_Vendor_ORB -> rundown ((CORBA::Flags) 0, ev);
    exit(0);
    }

// Get the Department object from the file using the employee name
// passed in
temp_file . open (argv[1], ios::in);
if (!temp_file)
    {
    cerr << "Could not open File " << argv[1] <<
      " to get Department object reference" << endl;
    exit(0);
    }
temp_file >> string_obj;
if (!temp_file)
    {
    cerr <<
      "Could not read the Department object reference from the file"
      << endl;
    exit(0);
    }
temp_file . close();

// Convert the string-formatted Department object reference to a
// binary-formatted object reference

dep_obj_ptr = CORBA_Vendor_ORB -> string_to_object (
                                   string_obj,
                                   ev);
```

(continued on next page)

**Example A–3 (Cont.) Example Client Application, Client_main.cxx**

```
if ((ev . exception()) || (CORBA::is_nil(dep_obj_ptr, ev)))
    {
    ev . clear();
    CORBA::release (dep_obj_ptr, ev );
    CORBA_Vendor_ORB -> rundown ((CORBA::Flags) 0, ev);
    exit(0);
    }
// Narrow the CORBA::Object to a CORP::Department object reference
dep_obj = CORP::Department::_narrow(dep_obj_ptr);

if (!dep_obj)
    {
    ev . clear();
    CORBA::release (dep_obj_ptr, ev );
    CORBA_Vendor_ORB -> rundown ((CORBA::Flags) 0, ev);
    exit(0);
    }
// Fill out the emp_data argument
emp_data . last_name = argv[2];
emp_data . first_name = argv[3];
emp_data . middle_name = argv[4];
emp_data . job_class = * argv[5];
emp_data . hourly_rate = atof(argv[6]);

// Hire the employee
emp_obj = pers_obj -> hire(emp_data, dep_obj, badge_num, ev);
if (ev . exception())
    {
    cout << "Could not hire the employee" << endl;
    ev . clear();
    CORBA::release(dep_obj_ptr, ev);
    CORBA::release(pers_obj_ptr, ev);
    CORBA::release(dep_obj, ev);
    CORBA::release(pers_obj, ev);
    CORBA_Vendor_ORB -> rundown ((CORBA::Flags) 0, ev);
    exit( 0 );
    }
```

(continued on next page)

**Example A–3 (Cont.)  Example Client Application, Client_main.cxx**

```
// Get the employee's data to verify the data is correct
emp_data = emp_obj -> get_EmpData(ev);
if (ev . exception())
    {
    cerr << "Could not get the employee data" << endl;
    ev . clear();
    CORBA::release(dep_obj_ptr, ev);
    CORBA::release(pers_obj_ptr, ev);
    CORBA::release(emp_obj, ev);
    CORBA::release(dep_obj, ev);
    CORBA::release(pers_obj, ev);
    CORBA_Vendor_ORB -> rundown ((CORBA::Flags) 0, ev);
    exit(0);
    }

// Echo the employee data back to the end user
cout << "Hiring process complete for employee:" << endl;
cout << "\tLast Name : \t" << emp_data . last_name << endl;
cout << "\tFirst Name : \t", emp_data . first_name << endl;
cout << "\tMiddle Name : \t", emp_data . middle_name << endl;
cout << "\tJob Class : \t", emp_data . job_class << endl;
cout << "\tHourly Rate: ", emp_data . hourly_rate << endl;

// Release all memory associated with emp_data argument
CORBA::free(emp_data . last_name);
CORBA::free(emp_data . first_name);
CORBA::free(emp_data . middle_name);

// Release all the objects
CORBA::release(pers_obj_ptr, ev);
CORBA::release(dep_obj_ptr, ev);
CORBA::release(emp_obj, ev);
CORBA::release(dep_obj, ev);
CORBA::release(pers_obj, ev);
if (ev . exception())
exit(0);
}
```

# B

# Names of CORBA Operations and Objects for Versions 1.1 and 1.2

Version 1.1 of *The Common Object Request Broker: Architecture and Specification* did not specify the scoping for the names of the CORBA operations and objects the way that user-defined operations and objects are to be scoped.

In Version 1.2 of this specification, it was decided that to avoid name clashes with other programming languages or software systems, all CORBA-defined names would be scoped as if they occurred in the module CORBA. This means that all the names defined within the CORBA specification, such as keywords, operation names, and so on, are scoped using the same rules as user-defined names. In this book, we use the fully scoped Version 1.2 names to avoid ambiguity, and to be in compliance with the Version 1.2 specification.

Table B–1 lists the CORBA object names used in the Version 1.1 specification and the fully scoped C binding of those names as found in the Version 1.2 specification.

**Table B–1   Changes in CORBA Object Names**

| Nonscoped Name from CORBA 1.1 Specification | Fully Scoped Name from CORBA 1.2 Specification |
| --- | --- |
| BOA | CORBA_BOA |
| Context | CORBA_Context |
| NVList | CORBA_NVList |
| Object | CORBA_Object |
| ORB | CORBA_ORB |
| Request | CORBA_Request |

# Names of CORBA Operations and Objects for Versions 1.1 and 1.2

Table B–2 lists the CORBA operation names used in the 1.1 specification and the fully scoped C binding of those names as found in the 1.2 specification.

**Table B–2   Changes in CORBA Operation Names**

| Nonscoped Name from CORBA 1.1 Specification | Fully Scoped Name from CORBA 1.2 Specification |
| --- | --- |
| BOA_change_implementation | CORBA_BOA_change_implementation |
| BOA_create | CORBA_BOA_create |
| BOA_deactivate_impl | CORBA_BOA_deactivate_impl |
| BOA_deactivate_obj | CORBA_BOA_deactivate_obj |
| BOA_dispose | CORBA_BOA_dispose |
| BOA_get_id | CORBA_BOA_get_id |
| BOA_get_principal | CORBA_BOA_get_principal |
| BOA_impl_is_ready | CORBA_BOA_impl_is_ready |
| BOA_obj_is_ready | CORBA_BOA_obj_is_ready |
| BOA_set_exception | CORBA_BOA_set_exception |
| Context_create_child | CORBA_Context_create_child |
| Context_delete | CORBA_Context_delete |
| Context_delete_values | CORBA_Context_delete_values |
| Context_get_values | CORBA_Context_get_values |
| Context_set_one_value | CORBA_Context_set_one_value |
| Context_set_values | CORBA_Context_set_values |
| NVList_add_item | CORBA_NVList_add_item |
| NVList_free | CORBA_NVList_free |
| NVList_free_memory | CORBA_NVList_free_memory |
| NVList_get_count | CORBA_NVList_get_count |
| Object_create_request | CORBA_Object_create_request |
| Object_duplicate | CORBA_Object_duplicate |
| Object_get_implementation | CORBA_Object_get_implementation |
| Object_get_interface | CORBA_Object_get_interface |
| Object_is_nil | CORBA_Object_is_nil |
| Object_release | CORBA_Object_release |

(continued on next page)

**Table B–2 (Cont.)  Changes in CORBA Operation Names**

| Nonscoped Name from CORBA 1.1 Specification | Fully Scoped Name from CORBA 1.2 Specification |
|---|---|
| ORB_create_list | CORBA_ORB_create_list |
| ORB_create_operation_list | CORBA_ORB_create_operation_list |
| ORB_get_default_context | CORBA_ORB_get_default_context |
| ORB_object_to_string | CORBA_ORB_object_to_string |
| ORB_string_to_object | CORBA_ORB_string_to_object |
| Request_add_arg | CORBA_Request_add_arg |
| Request_delete | CORBA_Request_delete |
| Request_get_response | CORBA_Request_get_response |
| Request_invoke | CORBA_Request_invoke |
| Request_send | CORBA_Request_send |
| get_next_response | CORBA_get_next_response[1] |
| ORBfree | CORBA_free[1] |
| send_multiple_requests | CORBA_send_multiple_requests[1] |

[1]This operation is defined in *The Common Object Request Broker: Architecture and Specification* as a C routine rather than an IDL operation, and so no IDL interface name, such as Request, is part of the name.

# C

# CORBA Standard Exceptions

Table C–1 lists the standard exceptions specified by CORBA and their meanings. For more information on using standard exceptions, see Chapter 7.

**Table C–1  Standard Exceptions**

| Exception | Description |
|---|---|
| BAD_CONTEXT | There has been an error processing the context object. |
| BAD_INV_ORDER | The routine invocations are out of order. |
| BAD_OPERATION | The operation used was not valid. |
| BAD_PARAM | The parameter passed was not valid. |
| BAD_TYPECODE | The TypeCode used was not valid. |
| COMM_FAILURE | There has been a communication failure. |
| DATA_CONVERSION | There has been a data conversion error. |
| FREE_MEM | Memory cannot be freed. |
| IMP_LIMIT | The implementation limit has been violated. |
| INITIALIZE | ORB initialization has failed. |
| INTERNAL | There has been an internal ORB error. |
| INTF_REPOS | There has been an error in accessing the interface repository. |
| INV_FLAG | The flag specified was not valid. |
| INV_IDENT | The identifier syntax specified was not valid. |
| INV_OBJREF | The object reference is invalid. |
| MARSHAL | There has been an error in marshaling a parameter or result. |
| NO_IMPLEMENT | The operation implementation is unavailable. |

(continued on next page)

# CORBA Standard Exceptions

**Table C–1 (Cont.)   Standard Exceptions**

| Exception | Description |
|-----------|-------------|
| NO_MEMORY | Dynamic memory allocation has failed. |
| NO_PERMISSION | There is no permission for the attempted operation. |
| NO_RESOURCES | There were insufficient resources for the request. |
| NO_RESPONSE | A response to the request is not yet available. |
| OBJ_ADAPTER | The object adapter has detected a failure. |
| PERSIST_STORE | An attempt at persistent storage has failed. |
| TRANSIENT | There has been a transient failure; reissue the request. |
| UNKNOWN | The exception is unknown. |

# D

# Summary of Operations for Dynamic Invocation

This appendix summarizes the operations and C language routines for creating a dynamic invocation of a request. The descriptions in this appendix contain background information on the operations and what they do; however, the descriptions are not intended to be full descriptions of how to use or specify these operations. Your CORBA vendor should provide detailed information on these operations and their use.

### CORBA_get_next_response

Is a C routine, not an operation, that is used to obtain the next completed response for deferred synchronous requests. This routine is very similar to the CORBA_Request_get_response operation, except that instead of checking or waiting until a specified request has completed, it checks or waits until any request has completed.

Despite the name of this operation, there is no guarantee in the ordering of completed requests. The order in which responses are returned from successive CORBA_get_next_response calls is not necessarily related to the order in which they were completed.

If this routine indicates that the operation is complete, then the out parameters and the return values defined in the request may be used as if they had been synchronously invoked using the CORBA_Request_invoke operation.

If this routine is specified using the RESP_NO_WAIT response flag, and there are no completed requests pending, then the routine returns immediately. You may want to use this flag if you are using the CORBA_get_next_response routine in a loop and do not want to wait for it to return. You may also be able to use this flag to manually synchronize deferred synchronous calls.

### CORBA_NVList_add_item

Adds a new item to the specified list after the last added item.

## Summary of Operations for Dynamic Invocation

**CORBA_NVList_free**

Frees a list structure and any memory associated with it. This operation makes an implicit call to the CORBA_NVList_free_memory operation to do its work.

**CORBA_NVList_free_memory**

Frees any dynamically allocated output argument memory associated with a list structure. The list structure itself is not freed.

**CORBA_NVList_get_count**

Returns the total numbers of items allocated for the specified list.

**CORBA_Object_create_request**

Creates a request object. If an argument list is specified, that argument list is associated with the request to be created. If an argument list is omitted (specified as NULL), any arguments must be specified using the CORBA_Request_add_arg operation.

**CORBA_ORB_create_list**

Creates a list object, allocates a list of a specified size, and initializes that list. Items may be added to this list using the CORBA_NVList_add_item operation or by indexing directly into the list structure; however, you may not mix these two approaches.

**CORBA_ORB_create_operation_list**

Creates a list that is initialized with the arguments described. The arguments are returned in the same order as they were defined. The CORBA_NVList_free operation is used to free the returned information.

**CORBA_Request_add_arg**

Incrementally adds arguments to a request. Each argument added must include at least the argument's value and length; however, the argument's data type, name and usage flags may also be specified.

**CORBA_Request_delete**

Deletes a request object and frees any memory associated with the request object.

**CORBA_Request_get_response**

Is used to determine whether a deferred synchronous request is completed. When this operation is used, it waits until it receives a notification that a particular operation is complete. Once it receives this notification that the operation is complete, the out parameters and the return values defined in the request may be used as if they had been synchronously invoked using the CORBA_Request_invoke operation.

If this operation is specified using the RESP_NO_WAIT response flag, then the CORBA_Request_get_response operation returns immediately, even if the request it is attempting to get a response from is still in progress. You may want to use this flag if you are using the CORBA_Request_get_response operation in a loop and do not want to have to wait for it to return. You may be able to use this flag to manually synchronize deferred synchronous calls.

## CORBA_Request_invoke

Invokes a synchronous request. This operation waits for a response to the request before returning control to the calling program. The response to the request is stored in the same CORBA_NVList that was passed in. The program then reads this list to get the information out.

## CORBA_Request_send

Invokes a single deferred synchronous request. This operation returns to the calling program without waiting for a response. If not specified using the one-way attribute and if the invocation flag INV_NO_RESPONSE was not specified, this operation requires that the programmer poll for when the request completes using the CORBA_Request_get_response operation or CORBA_get_next_response routine. If one-way or INV_NO_RESPONSE was not specified, the raises clause can be used to return operation-specific error messages.

If specified using the one-way operation attribute or the request invocation flag INV_NO_RESPONSE, this operation does not require that the programmer poll for the response, since these indicate that no response should be returned and that no in or inout arguments will be updated. Specifying the INV_NO_RESPONSE response flag has the same effect as specifying the requested operation with the one-way attribute.

## CORBA_send_multiple_requests

Is a C routine, not an operation, that invokes multiple deferred synchronous requests. These requests are passed into the routine as an array of request objects. The execution order of these requests will depend on your vendor's CORBA system. Such an array of requests might be used to notify multiple applications of some event using a single operation. In addition, this routine may be useful for applications running in a thread-safe CORBA system.

Like CORBA_Request_send, this routine returns to the calling program without waiting for a response, and requires that the program poll for when the requests complete by using the CORBA_get_response operation or the CORBA_get_next_response routine. Also, like CORBA_Request_send, the one-way attribute and the INV_NO_RESPONSE invocation flag are valid and have the same meanings.

## Summary of Operations for Dynamic Invocation

In addition, the INV_TERM_ON_ERR invocation flag can be set to indicate that if one of the requests causes an error, the remaining unsent requests should not be sent.

# Glossary

**abstract model**

A simplified representation of something real that is more complex. Creating an abstract model of an activity or a thing helps you better understand the activity or thing you are modeling.

*See also* **abstraction** and **modeling**.

**abstraction**

A mental process and a software design technique in which a group of items is thought about in a more general way, so as to make useful generalizations about those items.

*See also* **information hiding**.

**activation**

The process of preparing an object to execute operations. For example, stored data might be copied into the implementation's memory to allow execution of methods on the stored data.

*See also* **activation policy**.

**activation policy**

One of a set of rules that describe how a given implementation behaves when there are multiple objects or implementations active. There are four activation policies that must be supported by the BOA.

*See also* **BOA**.

**application framework**

Software that provides the infrastructure that makes it possible for sets of applications or other software components to work together.

## API

Application Programming Interface. In traditional programming, a set of calls that you use to call services that are external to the program.

## Application Programming Interface

*See* **API**.

## asynchronous communication

A form of communication where one piece of software sends a message to another piece of software and then continues working, and retrieves the reply to the message at some later time. CORBA calls its asynchronous communication style deferred synchronous.

*See also* **deferred synchronous communication** and **synchronous communication**, and **one-way communication**.

## Basic Object Adapter

*See* **BOA**.

## BOA

Basic Object Adapter. An object adapter that must be supplied as part of a CORBA system. The BOA, as its name implies, is designed to be the most basic and most commonly used object adapter and connects the ORB to the server through server skeletons or other mechanisms.

*See also* **object adapter**, **ORB**, and **server skeleton**.

## broker

Software that provides the intelligence to map abstract service requests from the client to a particular server implementation.

*See also* **request**.

## client

In CORBA, the software that requests a task to be performed for it by a server. In client/server terminology, a client application typically contains the user interface, as opposed to the server, which typically stores and manipulates the data.

*See also* **server**.

### client/server

A distribution model in which there are two types of applications: client applications that request that tasks be performed and server applications that perform those tasks.

*See also* **client** and **server**.

### client stub

A language-specific mapping of OMG IDL operation definitions for an object type (defined by an interface) into procedural routines, one for each operation. A client stub maps OMG IDL operation definitions for an object type (defined by an interface definition) into procedural routines that will be called to invoke a request.

*See also* **IDL** and **stub-style invocation**.

### closed framework

A framework that does not allow you to remove and replace software components easily in a "plug-and-play" fashion.

*See also* **application framework** and **open framework**.

### Common Object Request Broker Architecture

*See* **CORBA**.

### computer downsizing

The process of moving your business from non-distributed computing on mainframe computers in computer labs to distributed computing between workstations and personal computers in your offices.

*See also* **computer upsizing**.

### computer upsizing

The process of moving your business from non-distributed computing on individual personal computers to networked distributed computing that includes individual personal computers, high performance server personal computers, and workstations.

*See also* **computer downsizing**.

### context object

A CORBA component that represents information about the client, environment, or circumstances of a request that for some reason are not passed as parameters to the request. A context object contains a list of properties each consisting of a name and a string value associated with that name.

*See also* **request**.

### CORBA

Common Object Request Broker Architecture. An architecture and a specification for distributed object-oriented computing that has implementations currently available from several major software vendors.

### deactivation

The process of releasing an object, so that it can no longer accept requests.

*See also* **activation**.

### deferred synchronous communication

The name CORBA uses for its asynchronous communication style.

*See also* **asychronous communication, synchronous communication**, and **one-way communication**.

### deployment

The process of placing an application in a distributed environment and making it available for use. Deployment can include such tasks as installation, configuration, and administration of various parts of the application.

### direction attribute

An OMG IDL attribute that indicates the direction in which the argument is to be passed between the client and server. This is similar to a passing mode in most programming languages. In, out, and inout are valid direction attributes.

*See also* **IDL**.

### distributed object computing

The combination of distributed computing with object-oriented computing. CORBA is an example of distributed object computing.

## dynamic invocation

A form of invocation in which the the request is not completely constructed until run time. Dynamic invocation uses the interface repository to get the signature of your object's operations at run time.

*See also* **invocation, interface repository,** and **signature.**

## encapsulation

A software technique in which data is packaged together with its corresponding procedures. In CORBA terms, the object is the mechanism for encapsulation.

## exception

An exception is signaled by either the ORB or by the implementation to indicate that a request was not successfully performed. Both standard and user exceptions can be defined and they are stored in the environment argument to a request.

*See also* **implementation, ORB,** and **request.**

## framework

*See* **application framework.**

## graphical user interface

*See* **GUI.**

## GUI

Graphical user interface. An interface to a piece of software that makes use of graphical entities, such as menus, windows, and so on. Most PC applications have graphical user interfaces.

## IDL

Interface Definition Language. A definition language that is used in CORBA to describe an object's interface; that is, the characteristics and behavior of a kind of object, including the operations that can be performed on those objects.

*See also* **interface.**

## implementation

A CORBA component that satisfies a client's request for an operation on a specific object (the object and associated operation are defined by the object's interface). An implementation exists in a server and contains one or more methods, which are the pieces of code that actually do the work requested of the implementation.

*See also* **interface**, **method**, and **server**.

### Implementation repository

A storage place for implementation definitions, just as an interface repository is a storage place for interface definitions.

*See also* **implementation** and **interface repository**.

### Implementation spreading

The ability of an implementation that supports an interface to be separated into several parts, with each part of the implementation potentially being in a separate server.

Implementation spreading is not required by CORBA and might be available only from certain vendors.

*See also* **implementation** and **interface**.

### Information hiding

A software design technique in which a piece of code contains only the information it needs to do its job. In structured programming, information hiding is used when you make the variables used by a certain function local to that function instead of making the variables available globally throughout the module or program.

*See also* **abstraction**.

### Inheritance

The ability of an object to inherit behavior from one or more interfaces. When an object inherits behavior from a single interface, it is called single inheritance. When an object inherits behavior from more than one interface, it is called multiple inheritance.

*See also* **interface**.

### Instance

A term used in object-oriented systems to indicate that something is a specific occurrence of a more general case. For example, you are a specific instance of the general concept of a person, and the chair you are now sitting in is a specific instance of the general concept of chair.

### Interaction model

Describes how the clients and servers in your distributed application or application framework work with each other.

### interface

Defines the characteristics and behavior of a kind of object, including the operations that can be performed on those objects. Interfaces are defined in CORBA using OMG IDL.

*See also* **IDL.**

### interface definition

A description of the attributes and operations that can be performed on an object. You use OMG IDL to create interface definitions in CORBA. Also known as an object description.

### interface inheritance

*See* **inheritance.**

### Interface Definition Language

*See* **IDL.**

### interface repository

A CORBA system component that acts as a storage place for modules of interface information, such as the interface definitions you code in the OMG IDL language.

*See also* **IDL.**

### invocation

In CORBA, the process of making a request for an operation on an object from the client to the server. CORBA supports two forms of invocation: stub-style invocation and dynamic invocation.

*See also* **stub-style invocation** and **dynamic invocation.**

### life cycle

The progress of software from requirements specification, design, implementation, and testing to product development and later to product retirement. The life cycle of a CORBA object starts with the creation of the object, followed by object activation, object implementation, object deactivation, and finally object destruction..

*See also* **object.**

### message

*See* **request.**

**method**

The code contained in an implementation that actually accomplishes a client's request for an operation on a specific object. Methods associated with an object can be a single piece of a program's capabilities or a combination of many programs' functions.

*See also* **implementation**.

**middleware**

Services for building distributed client/server applications, such as services for locating other programs in the network, establishing communication with them, passing information between applications, overcoming disparities between different computing platforms, and providing a uniform security model in a multivendor, multi-operating system network.

**modeling**

A design technique used in developing architecture, simulations, and in this case, computer systems.

*See also* **abstract model**.

**multiple inheritance**

*See* **inheritance**.

**object**

An entity that can have actions, called operations, performed on it. An object is defined by its interface.

*See also* **interface** and **operation**.

**object adapter**

A CORBA system component provided by the CORBA vendor to handle general ORB-related tasks, such as activating objects, activating implementations, and so on. The server skeleton takes these general tasks and ties them to particular implementations and methods in the server. The Basic Object Adapter (BOA) is the most commonly used object adapter.

*See also* **BOA**, **implementation**, and **server skeleton**.

### object attribute

A technique used to model data that is associated with an object. This data is described by the value of the object attribute. For example, if we had an object attribute named employee_badge, the value of employee_badge would be the employee's badge number, such as 1239.

An object attribute can have one or two functions defined for it, depending on how it is declared: one function to retrieve (get) the value of the object attribute and one function to enter (set) the value of the object attribute.

*See also* **operation** and **object**.

### object implementation

*See* **implementation**.

### object reference

Indicates a specific object to the CORBA system.

*See also* **object**.

### Object Request Broker

*See* **ORB**.

### OMG IDL

*See* **IDL**.

### one-way communication

A communication style in which a request is sent, but no response is expected or checked for. One-way requests are invoked on operations that are defined with the OMG IDL oneway attribute.

*See also* **deferred synchronous communication** and **synchronous communication**.

### open framework

A framework that allows you to remove and replace software components easily in a "plug-and-play" fashion.

*See also* **application framework** and **closed framework**.

## operation

An action that can be performed on an object, given a specified set of arguments.

*See also* **object**.

## ORB

Object Request Broker. A CORBA system component that acts as an intermediary between requests sent from clients to servers.

*See also* **client**, **request**, and **server**.

## polymorphism

The ability of two or more classes of objects to respond to the same message, each in its own way.

## principal object

An object within CORBA that contains information on who issued a request for an operation. This information can be accessed for authentication and access control purposes by using the `CORBA_BOA_get_principal` operation.

## pseudo object

Object references that cannot be transmitted across the network. Psuedo objects are similar to other objects, but because the ORB owns them, they cannot be extended. Pseudo objects include the ORB, BOA, context object, environment object, request, TypeCode, principal object, and NVList.

## Remote Procedure Call

*See* **RPC**.

## request

A message in a CORBA system that is sent from a client to a server. A CORBA request is invoked to accomplish an operation on a specific object.

## RPC

Remote Procedure Call. A procedural communication mechanism used between applications.

## server

A piece of software that performs some task that is requested of it by a client. In client/server terminology, a server application typically stores and manipulates the data, as opposed to the client, which contains the user interface.

*See also* **client**.

## server skeleton

A language-specific mapping of OMG IDL operation definitions for an object type (defined by an interface) into procedural routines that will be called by the skeleton when a corresponding request arrives.

*See also* **interface** and **request**.

## signature

A programming term for the arguments associated with a routine or operation. In CORBA, the signature for an operation includes the arguments that are part of that specific operation, including their order, data types, direction attribute, result (if any), and possible outcome.

*See also* **operation** and **direction attribute**.

## state

A description (typically in memory) of the current situation of an object.

*See also* **object**.

## stub

*See* **client stub**.

## stub-style invocation

A form of invocation in which the request is fully constructed when you generate your client stubs, including the signature of your object's operations.

*See also* **client stub** and **invocation**.

## synchronous communication

A form of communication where one piece of software sends a message to another piece of software and then waits for a reply. The software cannot perform any other tasks until it receives this reply.

*See also* **asynchronous communication**.

# Index

Invocation
    communication styles for,  8–4
    dynamic,  3–9, 8–13, 8–14 to 8–19, 8–45
    selecting type of,  8–7, 11–3
    stub-style,  3–8, 8–7 to 8–12
INV_NO_RESPONSE flag,  8–7

# L

Legacy application,  4–2, 9–9
    encapsulation of,  9–12, 9–18
Linking,  2–1, 3–19, 6–5
ls command,  8–24

# M

_major member
    *See* Exceptions
Management of objects
    BOA operations for,  9–2
    by implementations,  9–9, 9–10
    object adapters for,  9–1
    user-routines for,  9–7
Memory management,  8–20, 8–54, 9–22
Methods,  2–4, 9–19
    access control with,  9–25
    authentication with,  9–25
    BOA API with,  3–5
    code for,  9–7, 9–19
    creating object references with,  9–20
    defining,  10–1
    form of,  9–19
    getting reference data for,  9–22
    handling exceptions in,  9–23
    spreading across implementations,  10–6
Middleware,  1–14, 1–15
Minor code
    *See* Exceptions
Model
    abstract,  4–7
    applications of,  6–12
    broker interaction,  6–8
    comparison of object-oriented and
        data-centered,  4–11
    convenience functions,  6–4

Model (cont'd)
    converting abstract to object,  4–9
    data in,  7–4
    data interaction of,  6–2
    for distributed objects,  6–2
    interaction,  6–5 to 6–14
    interface abstraction in,  6–2
    object,  4–9
    peer-to-peer,  6–6
    real-world,  5–1
    refining,  6–1
    representing in IDL code,  4–11
    selection of,  6–14
    user interaction of,  6–2
    using for application design,  4–4 to 4–12
Modules
    description of,  A–1
    example of,  7–2, 7–11, A–1
    in interface repository,  3–4
    inheritance across,  7–11, 7–13

# N

Naming of operations,  B–1
Network transports,  4–3

# O

Object
    and inheritance,  5–4
    attributes of,  5–7 to 5–9, 7–4
    context,  3–11, 8–2
    creating,  5–3, 7–4, 9–3, 9–26, 11–5
    description of,  7–2
    factory,  6–13
    implementation of,  2–4, 9–4
    initial,  5–3, 9–26, 11–3, 11–5
    instance of,  2–4, 9–4, 9–9
    interface,  7–2, 9–4
    life cycle,  9–3
    management of
        *See* Management of objects
    operations on,  3–15, 5–2, 5–3, 5–7
    principal,  9–25
    pseudo,  3–8, 3–10, 8–2